KU-373-738

MALTA & GOZO

BY
SUSIE BOULTON

AA

Produced by AA Publishing

Written by Susie Boulton

Original photography by Philip Enticknap

Edited, designed and produced by AA Publishing. Maps ©
The Automobile Association 1994

Distributed in the United Kingdom by AA Publishing, Norfolk
House, Priestley Road, Basingstoke, Hampshire, RG24 9NY.

The contents of this publication are believed correct at the
time of printing. Nevertheless, the publishers cannot be held
responsible for any errors or omissions or for changes in the
details given in this guide or for the consequences of any
reliance on the information provided by the same. Assessments
of attractions, hotels, restaurants and so forth are based upon
the author's own experience and, therefore, descriptions given
in this guide necessarily contain an element of subjective opinion which
may not reflect the publishers' opinion or dictate a reader's own
experiences on another occasion.
**We have tried to ensure accuracy in this guide, but things do
change and we would be grateful if readers would advise us of any
inaccuracies they may encounter.**

A CIP catalogue record for this book is available from the British
Library.

ISBN 0 7495 0694 6

Published by AA Publishing (a trading name of Automobile Association
Developments Limited, whose registered office is Norfolk House,
Priestley Road, Basingstoke, Hampshire RG24 9NY. Registered number
1878835) and the Thomas Cook Group Ltd.

Colour separation: Daylight Colour Art PTE, Singapore

Printed by Edicoes ASA, Oporto, Portugal

Cover picture: *Spinola Bay, St Julian's*
Title page: *Fortifications at Senglea*
Above: *Shopping in Mdina*

Contents

About this Book

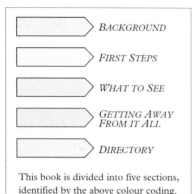

BACKGROUND

FIRST STEPS

WHAT TO SEE

GETTING AWAY FROM IT ALL

DIRECTORY

This book is divided into five sections, identified by the above colour coding.

Background gives an introduction to the country – its history, geography, politics, culture.

First Steps offers practical advice on arriving and getting around.

What to See is an alphabetical listing of places to visit, interspersed with walks and tours.

Getting Away From it All highlights places off the beaten track where it's possible to relax and enjoy peace and quiet.

Finally, the **Directory** provides practical information – from shopping and entertainment to children and sport, including a section on business matters.

Special highly illustrated features on specific aspects of the country appear throughout the book.

Sunday market, Valletta

BACKGROUND

'Malta – that tiny rock of history and romance.'

WINSTON CHURCHILL,
The Second World War, 1948

Introduction

*M*alta and Gozo draw over a million visitors a year. Tiny though it is, Malta has an extraordinarily rich historical and cultural heritage. Set at the crossroads of numerous Mediterranean sea routes, it has been coveted and colonised by many different maritime powers. The most glorious phase in its history was the 268-year reign of the Order of St John, whose legacy can still be seen in the fine buildings that survive.

The first impression, if you come in summer, is of a dry, barren, treeless rock. The other striking factor is the scale of the development which spreads out in all directions. Conscious of this the island is now working hard to boost its image. Many 4- and 5-star hotels are being renovated and all new hotel construction has been halted.

Gozo, meanwhile, carries on at its own gentle pace. If peace and solitude are priorities, this smaller, greener island provides the perfect escape.

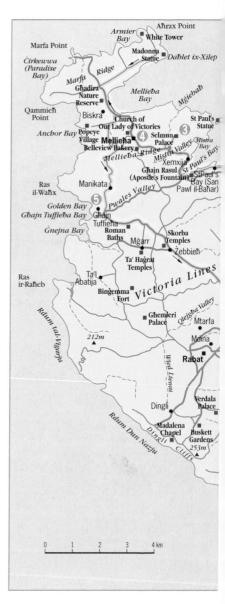

MALTA

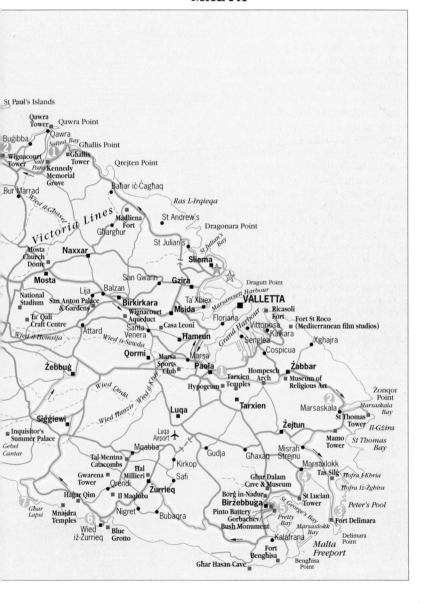

History

Around 5000BC
Neolithic farmers arrive.
5000–4000BC
Neolithic period. Skorba Temples built.
4000–3000BC
Temple Period. Age of Tarxien and Ġgantija temples and Ħal Saflieni Hypogeum.
2500–700BC
Bronze and Iron Age. Period of fortified villages and 'cart tracks'.
700–550BC
Phoenicians colonise the islands.
550–218BC
Period of Carthaginian rule.
218BC
Romans annexe Malta in their strategy to win the Second Punic War.
AD60
St Paul is shipwrecked on Malta and brings Christianity.
5th century
Roman power diminishes; Vandal raids.
6th century
Byzantine empire gains control.
870
The Arabs conquer Malta.
1090
Roger the Norman, ruler of Sicily and parts of southern Italy, takes Malta from the Arabs.
1194
Malta (with Sicily) becomes part of the German Hohenstaufen empire.
1266
Charles of Anjou takes over the kingdom of Sicily, of which Malta is part.
1282
Riots against French rule in Sicily. King Pedro I of Aragon defeats Charles of Anjou; Sicily and Malta come under the kingdom of Aragon.

mid-15th century
Emergence of a *università*, or local governing body, under Aragonese tutelage.
1429
Malta sacked by Muslims.
Early 16th century
Having declined economically and culturally, Malta is now little more than a rock with a population of about 20,000.
1530
Emperor Charles V of Spain grants the Maltese islands to the Knights of the Order of St John of Jerusalem. The Knights occupy the islands making Birgù (modern Vittoriosa) their headquarters.
1565
The Great Siege of Malta.
1566
The city of Valletta is founded.
1571
The Maltese capital is formally moved from Birgù to Valletta. A Christian fleet, assisted by the Knights, inflicts defeat on the Ottomans at Lepanto.
1676
Plague causes 8,569 deaths.
1693
Earthquake wrecks most of Mdina.
1735
Sicilian ports are closed to Maltese ships after Grand Master Vilhena resists Charles VIII's attempt to influence Maltese affairs.
Late 18th century
The Order becomes demilitarised and corrupted by wealth.
1792
The French National Assembly confiscates the Order's lands in France.

1798

Napoleon takes Malta and plunders the islands. The Order of St John is ordered to leave the island, obtaining a temporary home in Russia and later a headquarters in Rome. The Maltese rise up against the French; helped by the British, they besiege the main French garrison.

1800

The French capitulate and the British occupy the island.

1802

The Treaty of Amiens stipulates that Malta should be returned to the Knights, but a powerful group of Maltese declares allegiance to Britain.

1813

Sir Thomas Maitland is appointed as the first British Governor of Malta. Extensive constitutional and administrative reforms are made.

1814

The Treaty of Paris formally recognises Malta as a British Crown Colony.

1848

The British Admiralty's first dry dock is opened on the island.

1853–6

During the Crimean War, Malta acts as a strategic supply station for British forces.

1869

The opening of the Suez Canal makes Malta an important port on the British route to India.

1914–18

World War I. Malta becomes 'the Nurse of the Mediterranean', providing 25,000 beds for the wounded.

1921

Malta is granted self-government 'in matters of local concern'.

1940

Italy enters World War II and Malta suffers its first air raid.

1942

The Second Great Siege. Over 6,000 tonnes of bombs are dropped on Malta in April alone. On 15 April the George Cross is awarded to the Maltese people for their bravery during the air raids. In July the Maltese air force begins to gain control of its air space. In August and September, the German and Italian air forces suffer heavy losses over Malta and in October they concede defeat. The UK government announces a grant of £30 million for the reconstruction of the island.

1962

The State of Malta formally comes into being with Dr Borġ Olivier as its first Prime Minister.

1964

Malta is granted full independence within the British Commonwealth, though British forces remain.

1974

Malta is declared a republic.

1979

British forces finally leave Malta.

1989

Presidents Bush and Gorbachev meet on a ship moored off Malta for the so-called 'Seasick Summit'.

1990

Malta applies for full membership of the European Community.

Four Maltese were shot in the riots of 7 June 1919

7 TA GUNJU 1919

THE GREAT SIEGE

The Great Siege of Malta was one of the most remarkable military showdowns between Christian and Muslim, between the might of the Crescent and the forces of the Cross. In 1565 the Knights of St John, with some 9,000 men, defended the tiny island against a Turkish force of 40,000 and a fleet of 180 ships.

Well before the siege began it was common knowledge that Suleiman the Magnificent, the Sultan of Turkey, was planning to annihilate those 'sons of dogs'. Christendom was not united and for most of the four-month siege the Knights were left to go it alone. They were, however, renowned for their physical courage and, as the historian Edward Gibbons sardonically put it, they 'neglected to live, but were prepared to die, in the service of Christ'.

The Turkish commander, Piali Pasha, began the siege with an attack on Fort St Elmo. The defenders fought to the death, pouring down cauldrons of pitch and hoops of fire. The Turks eventually took the fort, but they lost 8,000 men to 1,500 Christians. The handful of surviving Knights were butchered, nailed to crosses and floated out of the Grand Harbour. Not to be outdone in barbarity, Grand Master La Valette ordered the severed heads of Turkish prisoners to be cannon-fired into the enemy camp.

The Turks then turned their attention to Birgù, mercilessly firing a

barrage at the buildings until they breached the fortress walls. Even so, their casualties were huge: on a single day they lost some 2,500 men. On 6 September the Viceroy of Sicily finally sent modest reinforcements to support

The Siege of Malta was viewed by all Europe as a major victory for Christianity in the fight against the Infidel

the Knights. The crafty La Valette released a Turkish prisoner, having tricked him into believing that the relief force was enormous. When this news was conveyed to the Muslims, it proved to be the last straw. Demoralised by fever and dysentery, they evacuated Malta on 8 September and sailed back to Constantinople, entering the city under cover of darkness out of shame.

The Christian world had watched with baited breath. Now, even the Protestant English Queen Elizabeth I gave orders for thanksgiving prayers to be said.

Geography

*T*he Maltese islands lie in the centre of the Mediterranean, 93km south of Sicily and 300km north of Libya. The archipelago is made up of the islands of Malta, Gozo and Comino, plus the tiny uninhabited islets of Cominotto in the north and Filfla, about 5km off the southern coast. Together the islands make up a mere 316sq km. Malta, the largest, is only 27km at its longest point from northwest to southeast, and 14.5km at its widest point, from west to east.

Climate

Malta's climate is typical of the Mediterranean, with long hot summers, warm and sporadically wet autumns and cool but unpredictable winters. Given that Malta lies south of Tunis, it is perhaps not surprising that it has an annual average of eight hours of sunshine a day.

Population

With a population of around 362,000, Malta is one of the most densely populated countries of Europe. However, the vast majority live in the Valletta conurbation.

Landscape

The island of Malta consists of a gently undulating limestone plateau. There are no mountains, rivers or lakes and the land looks rocky and barren, particularly in summer. This arid appearance is emphasised by the scores of drystone walls that flank fields, terraces, slopes, gardens and paths. To ease the water shortage, five reverse osmosis plants have been set up on the coast to convert seawater to fresh, and these now produce half of the water consumed on the island.

The Maltese woodlands were hacked down centuries ago and today the only trees you will see are the carob, pine, citrus, ficus and tamarisk that have been deliberately planted in public parks, along avenues and around town piazzas. On both Malta and Gozo the slopes are cultivated for vegetables and vines.

For centuries Malta's abundant limestone has been used for construction – from prehistoric megaliths to modern-day houses. Newly quarried stone soon mellows with exposure to the sun and blends with the colour of the surroundings. The most widely used limestone today is the soft globigerina.

Because of its greater quantity of water-retaining blue clay subsoil, Gozo is greener than Malta. The lie of the land is

Much of Malta consists of undulating limestone plateaux

Drystone walls surround tiny flower-filled fields in southern Malta

different, with villages built on flat-topped hills leaving the slopes for cultivation.

The coastline

The coastlines of Malta and Gozo are predominantly rocky, with only the very occasional sandy bay. Malta's coastline is heavily indented. The eastern side of the island is broken up by large bays which make ideal natural harbours. To the south spectacular cliffs drop 250m to the sea. Gozo's coastal scenery is at its most spectacular around the cliffs of Dwejra.

The economy

Tourism is Malta's prime industry, accounting for 30 per cent of the country's gross national product. In 1992 the number of visitors exceeded 1.2 million – well over three times the population of the islands. Ship-repair work still plays an important role in the economy and the newly established Malta Freeport is a major distribution centre, serving shipping and business markets.

Despite the thin dry soil, one of the mainstays of the economy is agriculture. The main vegetables are potatoes and onions. Grapes, the largest fruit crop, are made into wine for local consumption and for export.

THOMAS COOK'S MALTA

The opening of the Suez Canal in 1869 inspired Thomas Cook and his son to open an office in Cairo. Malta was a steamer stop en route to Egypt and 21 years later a Thomas Cook office was established here. Affluent British visitors began coming to Malta in the spring and autumn in search of the sun. The 20th century saw the arrival of summer holidaymakers and in the years following World War II, Malta started to develop its seaside resorts, becoming an important destination in the Thomas Cook summer brochures.

Culture

Malta's strategic setting at the crossroads of the Mediterranean shipping lanes has always played a crucial role in the island's history. Over the centuries the great Mediterranean powers have fought to dominate the islands, each new arrival leaving its legacy. What you see today is a complex amalgam of ethnic influences. The Arabs introduced citrus trees and the flat-topped houses and they laid the foundations for the Maltese language. The Aragonese, from central Spain, left their mark in the medieval architecture of Malta's historic town centres and the enclosed wooden balconies which typify the splendid town houses.

Architecture

Under the 268-year rule of the Knights of St John, Malta blossomed into a major cultural centre. The buildings they put

Cardinals, popes and St Paul are honoured in this religious festival

up touched on almost every sphere of human activity, from water distribution to heavy fortifications. By the time the British arrived at the start of the 19th century, Malta was at the forefront of European culture in terms of its architecture. In turn the British developed the island, both militarily and commercially.

The words which come most readily to mind in characterising Maltese architecture are religion, defence and limestone. Neolithic people left their mark in the mighty temples to their gods, while the long, continuous Christian tradition has given rise to huge and ever-more splendid edifices to the glory of God.

The island's defences are equally eloquent as can be seen in the siting of Arab Mdina or the fortifications of Aragonese Birgù (now Vittoriosa) or in the obsessive and interminable military building of the Knights. Malta is above all a fortress and the mighty defensive system, shoring up Valletta, Floriana and the Three Cities, is one of the greatest exhibitions of pre-modern Christian military architecture to be seen anywhere in the world.

The great architectural tool of all these builders was, and remains, the abundant honey-coloured globigerina limestone, easily cut and mellow to the eye.

Religion

Malta's long Christian tradition dates from AD60 when St Paul was shipwrecked on the island. In spite of Islamic and other cultural influences, Catholicism has always been a dominant force in Maltese life, influencing social, political and even economic issues. Around 87 per cent of Maltese are regular churchgoers – a higher percentage than in any other country in Europe. The village *festa*, celebrating the local patron saint, plays an essential role in cementing community spirit and there is intense rivalry between the different parishes who compete to mount the most spectacular parades and fireworks displays.

Further evidence of religious conviction is the abundance of street-corner shrines, from the finely carved to the crude and garishly coloured. Even some of the old-fashioned buses have a little shrine inside and a conspicuous *'Jesus loves me'* sticker beneath.

The churches of Malta and Gozo are primarily baroque in style. The great architect of the 16th century was Gerolamo Cassar (1526–86) who designed St John's Co-Cathedral in addition to the Knights' *auberges*, the fortifications and several other churches in Valletta. The 17th century saw the rise of another great Maltese architect, Lorenzo Gafà, whose work is best seen in the parish churches and cathedrals of Mdina and Gozo. Splendid domes are a hallmark of Maltese churches, their huge dimensions dwarfing the surrounding village houses. The interiors are grandiose, characterised by gilded arcades and ceilings, intricately ornate altars and

The Catholic religion is a dominant force in Maltese culture

canopies. Walls and vaults are covered in paintings and frescos, the principal exponent being the Italian master Mattia Preti, who decorated St John's Co-Cathedral and numerous other churches throughout Malta.

Arts and crafts

Malta's once-flagging arts and crafts industry has been given a big boost by tourism. Craft villages on both Malta and Gozo have been set up to demonstrate (and sell) all the traditional handicrafts. Though outside these villages the artisan is a dying breed, you can still occasionally glimpse a fisherman weaving cane into fish traps, a farmer's wife making baskets for eggs or an old woman skilfully making lace in the streets of southern Gozo.

Politics

*P*olitics in Malta is a serious business. Most people are politically aware and there is intense rivalry between the Nationalist and the Labour parties. It is not unusual for political differences to prevent a marriage taking place or for shops to be boycotted because their owners belong to the other party.

Since 1974 Malta has been a republic within the British Commonwealth. It has a single legislative chamber of 69 members, elected by proportional representation. The President is the constitutional Head of State; executive powers are held by the Parliament headed by the Prime Minister.

Under Dom Mintoff (who was Prime Minister from 1971 to 1984), Malta developed a stance of non-alignment in relation to the superpowers. He also provoked great controversy by fostering close links with Libya.

Vehement political slogans betray the bitterness of the 1987 election battle

In 1987, after 16 years of Labour rule, the Nationalists came to power. In the same year Malta's neutrality was incorporated into the constitution, but the government maintains a vigorous policy in favour of EC membership. An application for full membership was submitted by the National Party in July 1990. Rising standards of living and progressive growth led to the re-election of the Nationalists on 22 February 1992. While full EC membership remains the government's main objective, the reduction of the public sector, the monitoring of inflation and agreed wage increase guidelines are also important policy points.

FIRST STEPS

'There was something
about the appearance
of the people that
told you – here you are
in a place of safety.'

JOHN WEBSTER,
*Notes on a Journey from London to
Constantinople*, 1836

First Steps

Malta is a tiny island and – unless you are staying on the far northern or western side – you will be within easy striking distance of the main centres, museums and historic sites. Even so, the small size of the island can be deceptive: distances may be short, but the traffic – particularly through Valletta's seemingly endless conurbation and along the Sliema to Mellieħa coast road in summer – can severely hamper your journey.

Beaches

Maltese waters are among the bluest and cleanest in the Mediterranean – but sandy beaches are scarce. The main ones on Malta are Mellieħa Bay in the north, and the glorious golden beaches of Għajn Tuffieħa on the west coast. On Gozo the only sandy beach of any size is Ramla Bay, an extensive stretch of ochre-coloured sands.

Any sandy beach will be packed in season. Swimming and sunbathing otherwise take place at hotel pools or from the rocky shorelines. In some of the larger resorts, such as Sliema, artificial lidos provide good swimming, often from flattened rock ledges. The very best swimming is inevitably found away from the built-up areas and usually entails a

The leisurely way to explore Malta's rich cultural heritage

scramble down the cliffside. One of the loveliest spots of all is the Blue Lagoon off Comino – so long as you get there before the excursion boats.

The main beaches provide facilities such as cafés, sunbeds, parasols, showers and watersports. Amenities for scuba-diving are excellent. The only watersport you won't find in Malta is surfboarding.

Boat trips

Travelling by boat is one of the best ways of getting to know the island, whether by hopping on a local ferry, hiring a fisherman and his boat, or joining an organised cruise. A day in Gozo is worth it for the ferry trip alone. Organised tour options include a cruise around all the islands, an underwater safari or an underwater cruise by submarine. Don't take a boat trip on a particularly windy day.

Resorts

Malta's biggest tourist resort, Sliema, has abundant facilities and easy access to most parts of the island. Further north, tourist development has sprouted all around St Paul's Bay, stifling the old fishing village. Mellieħa and the resorts beyond it are somewhat remote but have good swimming and are handy for trips to Comino and Gozo.

The beautiful area of Għajn Tuffieħa on the west side of the island only has

Modern tower blocks mix with honey-coloured stone along Sliema Creek

one hotel at present. On the east side, the fishing village of Marsaskala is becoming increasingly popular as a resort, but picturesque Marsaxlokk remains very much a fishing village. In the south, high cliffs characterise the coastline, hence the absence of any development.

For a quiet time, opt for Gozo, which is still relatively free of the trappings of mass tourism. Quieter still is the tiny island of Comino, with just two hotels and only three permanent residents!

Sightseeing

In January 1993, museum and sight entrance fees rose by 560 per cent. The authorities argued that this merely brought them into line with the museums of other European countries (they were ludicrously low before). To soften the blow, entrance fees are waived on Sundays (except for the Hypogeum).

The main cultural centres of Malta are Valletta, Mdina and Rabat. The capital, Valletta, has sufficient museums, churches, palaces and bastions to keep you occupied for two or three days. Medieval Mdina is tiny but packs in a wealth of architecture and can be combined with a visit to the churches and catacombs of Rabat. Gozo's cultural hub is Victoria which has a fine citadel.

In the summer months avoid the midday heat by rising early to sightsee. From mid-June to the end of September, most sights on Malta open early (from 7.30am), then close at 1.45pm for the day. The exception is Gozo, where the sights are open all day.

THE BRITISH IN MALTA

'One felt the splendour of the British Empire, let the world say what it likes.'
D H LAWRENCE, 1924

After 160 years on Malta, it is not surprising that the British left their mark. British occupation began in 1800 (when Bridagier General Thomas Graham and his forces helped the Maltese drive out an occupying garrison of French Napoleonic soldiers) and it lasted until 1964, when Malta finally achieved independence.

The British legacy is apparent not so much in permanent monuments as in the little features of everyday Maltese life: the Bedford buses, the red pillar boxes and telephone kiosks, the curry served on Sundays at the Sports Club in Marsa.

Of course the British left big things as well: a constitution, a new legal system, a fine dockyards complex, a chain of forts and various monuments to British monarchs and worthies.

On the minus side the British created the first urban sprawl (spreading out from Valletta) and even considered knocking down the capital's ancient fortifications to make way for new housing. It was also British servicemen who named the red-light area of Valletta 'The Gut' and made it an institution.

Anglo-Maltese relations have improved since 1984 when Dom Mintoff stepped down as Prime Minister. The majority of Maltese still have a fondness for all things British – whether that means memories of the war, the football scene, roast beef or royalty. The Queen's visit in May 1992, planned to coincide with the 50th anniversary of the award to Malta of the George Cross, reaffirmed the links.

Given all this – and the fact that almost

everyone speaks English (because the British taught them to) – it comes as no surprise to learn that over 3,000 (one per cent) of Malta's residents are British and that of the million or so people who visit Malta every year, over half come from the United Kingdom.

For many years Malta was a strategic port and supply station for British forces and the legacy of British occupation is visible in many small details, from red post and telephone boxes to statues of Winston Churchill

The People

After centuries of foreign domination, it is not surprising that the Maltese are a resilient people. Towards visitors they are friendly and hospitable, though noticeably less ebullient than their Italian neighbours. Like all Latins, the Maltese are a proud nation. They respect the family and are crazy about children. Inevitably there are exceptions to the general *bonhomie*, notably the bus drivers (especially if you don't happen to have small change) and the occasional surly waiter.

Gozitans are slightly different from

After a long history of foreign domination, Maltese people are resilient

the Maltese and an amicable rivalry exists between the two islands. Gozitans, who, of necessity, have always been hardworking and thrifty, are accused by the Maltese of being pennypinching and go-getting. If this is true, it is certainly not apparent to the casual visitor. Gozitans seem every bit as friendly and hospitable as the Maltese.

Dress
Attitude towards dress is not as liberal as it is in some European countries. Topless bathing or sunbathing is against the law and may well offend the locals. In secluded spots, however, the law is frequently flouted. Sauntering around

streets or hotels in skimpy clothes or
swimwear is also frowned upon. As in
most Catholic countries the wearing of
mini-skirts, shorts or shoulderless
garments in churches is likely to cause
offence. It is particularly relevant to
respect this fact in a country where
religion is still the *raison d'être* of the local
community. Some of the most frequently
visited churches provide shawls and skirts
to cover offending parts – but nothing for
men, who are best advised to wear long
trousers and short-sleeved shirts for
church visiting.

In most restaurants and hotels dress is
smart but casual. The only place requiring
formal attire is the casino, where jacket
and tie are compulsory for men.

Language

Malta has two official languages – English
and Malti. Malti is a fascinating language,
reflecting a host of different influences. Its

The Maltese are linguistically adroit, speaking
both English and Malti

roots are Semitic and it was later modified
by the Arabs; then, under the rule of
various European powers, it took on a
smattering of Italian (mainly Sicilian),
Spanish, French and English.

The official language of the Order of
St John was Italian. Since Malti had no
written form (and at that stage was a very
basic language), literate Maltese tended to
speak Italian too. When the British
arrived they rather expected, in typical
British fashion, that local people would
simply drop Italian and pick up English
overnight. In fact it was not until 1921
that English became the official
administrative language.

Malti did not become a written
language until early this century. It is
written in modified Roman characters,
which seems incongruous for a language
that sounds so Arabic, and one in which
God is called Allah.

Today you can almost draw a
dividing line between the real Maltese
villages, where Malti is very much the
first language, and the more
sophisticated areas (such as Sliema)
where English is considered the superior
language and learnt from the cradle.
Between these two extremes are the
many Maltese who speak half and half.

For an English-speaking visitor to
Malta there is absolutely no need to try
and master the Maltese language. Signs
and notices are bilingual and the vast
majority of locals speak English, many of
them fluently, albeit with a very sing-
song intonation. The Maltese are good
linguists and many speak fluent Italian,
and French as well. Italian remains
popular because the Maltese have a
choice of over 15 Italian TV channels, so
children pick the language up easily.

Enjoying the pleasures of conversation in the open air

The Maltese lifestyle

In keeping with Mediterranean customs, most Maltese enjoy a siesta on summer afternoons. This lasts for two or three hours after lunch, during which time the majority of shops are closed. As a tourist you are best advised to follow suit and emerge again in the early hours of the evening, when the Maltese (again following the southern European habit) go out for an evening stroll, called the *passiġġata*.

Patriotism

With good reason the Maltese are passionately proud of their culture and history. On the other hand, living on a group of small islands has inevitably led to a certain insularity. While many Maltese, and particularly those who have travelled, are very cosmopolitan, others see their islands as the centre of the universe. This is despite the conspicuous influence of foreign cultures, and the strong links that are maintained with Maltese emigrants in the UK, Australia, the USA and Canada.

Women

Maltese society is still male-dominated and most women readily accept that their place is in the home (which is presumably why Maltese houses are always immaculate). Daughters are allowed far more freedom these days, but there is always a sigh of relief once a suitable marriage partner has been chosen – and once a woman is married, she ceases to have any legal authority over property or even her children! Such attitudes do not extend to non-Maltese women, and foreigners are unlikely to encounter anything more troublesome than the usual Mediterranean roving eye.

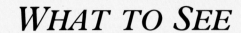

WHAT TO SEE

'*An epitome of all Europe.*'
PATRICK BRYDONE,
A Tour through Sicily and Malta, 1773

VALLETTA

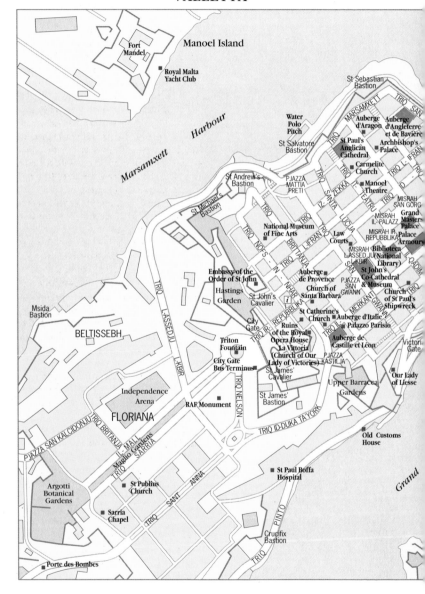

Fort Mandel

Manoel Island

Royal Malta Yacht Club

St Sebastian Bastion

Water Polo Pitch

Auberge d'Aragon

Auberge d'Angleterre et de Bavière

Archbishop's Palace

St Salvatore Bastion

St Paul's Anglican Cathedral

Harbour

Carmelite Church

Marsamxett

St Andrew's Bastion

Manoel Theatre

PJAZZA MATTIA PRETI

MISRAH SAN GORG

St Michael's Bastion

Grand Masters Palace

MISRAH IL-PALAZZ

National Museum of Fine Arts

MISRAH IR-REPUBBLIKA

Palace Armoury

Law Courts

MISRAH LASSED JU L-KBIR

Biblioteca (National Library)

Embassy of the Order of St John

Auberge de Provence

St John's Co-Cathedral & Museum

Hastings Garden

St John's Cavalier

Church of Santa Barbara

PJAZZA SAN GWANN

Church of St Paul's Shipwreck

Msida Bastion

St Catherine's Church

Auberge d'Italie

BELTISSEBH

City Gate

Ruins of the Royal Opera House

Auberge de Castille et Léon

Palazzo Parisio

Triton Fountain

La Vittoria (Church of Our Lady of Victories)

PJAZZA KASTILJA

Victoria Gate

City Gate Bus Terminus

St James' Cavalier

Independence Arena

St James' Bastion

Upper Barracca Gardens

Our Lady of Liesse

FLORIANA

RAF Monument

TRIQ ID-DUKA TA' YORK

Old Customs House

PJAZZA SAN KALCIDONJU

IL-MALL

Madio Gardens

St Paul Boffa Hospital

Grand

Argotti Botanical Gardens

St Publius Church

Sarria Chapel

Crucifix Bastion

Porte des Bombes

Valletta

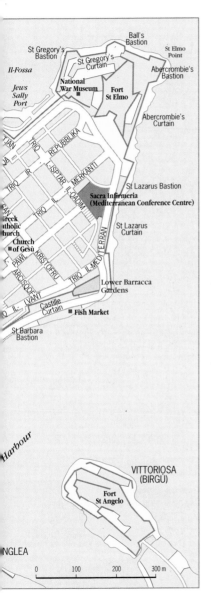

*I*t didn't take the Knights of St John long to discover the potential of the slopes of Mount Sceberras and the great sweep of surrounding harbour. A matter of months after the epic siege of 1565, Francesco Laparelli was sent to Malta by Pope Pius IV to advise on the building of a new city. The first stone was laid on 28 May 1566 and the city was completed by Laparelli's Maltese assistant, Gerolamo Cassar, just five years later. With the city complete, Cassar spent the next 20 years designing the various *auberges*, the residences for the Knights, as well as the Grand Masters' Palace and the great Co-Cathedral of St John.

Today the capital of Malta, Valletta is still the island's richest repository of art, architecture, history and culture. It is also the main shopping and business centre. Sightseeing could occupy two or three days, but equally rewarding are the walks round the ramparts or through the streets, many of which are still flanked by handsome balconied houses.

The main thoroughfare is Triq ir-Repubblika (Republic Street) which is full of shops and, during the morning and early evening, free of traffic. It cuts through the city before dropping down to Fort St Elmo on the tip of the peninsula. Leading off are numerous back streets forming a rectangular grid that has altered little over the years. Some of the narrowest slope very steeply down towards the harbour, and a glimpse of brilliant blue at the end of many streets reminds you that this is a very small city, almost entirely surrounded by water.

Few visitors to Malta make Valletta their base. Hotels are sparse and the city is quiet at night.

The *Auberges*

*T*he Order of St John was divided into eight *langues* (or nationalities), each one having its own *auberge*. Literally translated as an inn or hostel, this was more akin to an Oxford or Cambridge college, with a chapel, dining hall and accommodation ranged around a courtyard. Of the original *auberges*, five have survived and only two are open to the public. The exteriors alone, however, give you a good idea of the lifestyle enjoyed by the Knights.

The original eight *auberges* were first established in Birgù (now Vittoriosa). The Knights then moved to grander premises in Valletta when that city was built. By this time there were only seven *auberges*, Henry VIII having suppressed the English *langue* after his conjugal quarrel with the Pope.

All the *auberges* were built by Gerolamo Cassar between 1571 and 1590 though they were largely rebuilt

Cassar's Renaissance style Auberge d'Italie is now the General Post Office

during the 18th century. Each one differed in scale and style, reflecting the wealth of the Knights and the progressive gusto with which Cassar worked. The wealthiest of the Knights had their own lodgings, but dining in their *auberge* four times a week was compulsory. This presumably was no hardship since the *auberges* were well known for their high culinary standard. According to a 17th-century French writer: 'partridges, pigeons, rabbits, thrushes and other game (in Malta) are fatter than anywhere else in Europe'.

Of the *auberges* that no longer exist, the Auberge d'Allemagne (Pjazza Indipendenza/Independence Square) was pulled down to make way for St Paul's Anglican Cathedral; the Auberge d'Auvergne (Triq ir-Repubblika/Republic Street) was devastated by bombs in 1942 and replaced by the new Law Courts; and the Auberge de France (Triq Nofs-in-Nhar/South Street) – also the victim of bombs – was replaced by the General Workers' Union Headquarters.

Auberge d'Aragon
Built in 1571, this is the oldest and simplest of the *auberges*, a plain single-storey building facing St Paul's Anglican Cathedral. It is now used as government offices.
Pjazza Indipendenza (Independence Square). Not open.

Auberge d'Angleterre et de Bavière

Overlooking Marsamxett Harbour, this was originally the Palazzo Carnerio. It did not become the *auberge* of the Anglo-Bavarian *langue* until 1784 and only existed as such for 15 years. It is the least impressive of the surviving *auberges*.
On the English Curtain section of Triq San Bastjan (Bastion Road). Not open.

Auberge de Castille et Léon

Originally designed by Cassar, the Auberge de Castille et Léon was remodelled in 1744 for the Portuguese Grand Master Pinto. This libertine loved pomp and grandeur; of all the *auberges* (and arguably all the 18th-century buildings in Malta) this is the most magnificent. It is also the most Italianate of the *auberges*, based on the baroque architecture of Lecce in southern Italy. A flamboyant bust of Pinto, surrounded by trophies, banners and arms, adorns the façade. Once the headquarters of the British Army, the building is now the Prime Minister's office.
Pjazza Kastilja (Castille Place). Not open.

Auberge d'Italie

Now the General Post Office, the Auberge d'Italie has been substantially altered and enlarged since it was built in the late 16th century. It is typical of Cassar's work in its rustication and carved quoins.
Triq il-Merkanti (Merchants' Street). Post Office open: Monday to Saturday 7.45am–6pm (8am–6.30pm in winter).

Auberge de Provence

Founded in 1571, this *auberge* now houses the National Museum of Archaeology (see page 38). It was the most lavish *auberge* of them all, renowned for the excellence of its cuisine and its

The baroque Auberge de Castille et Léon, now the office of the Prime Minister

ornate rooms. The rich façade, possibly remodelled in the 17th century, is fronted by both Doric and Ionic columns.
Triq ir-Repubblika (Republic Street). Standard opening times (see page 185). Admission charge.

THE MALTESE CROSS

The eight-pointed cross, known as the Maltese Cross, symbolises the eight Beatitudes (as listed in Christ's Sermon on the Mount) and also the eight *langues* of the Order of St John: Allemagne (Germany), Aragon (Spain), Auvergne, England, France, Italy, Provence and Portugal. The four main sections of the cross symbolise the four Cardinal Virtues (Fortitude, Justice, Temperance and Perseverance). The white colour of the cross denotes purity, all the Knights being sworn to chastity, poverty and obedience.

Churches

*T*he Knights of St John, who combined the careers of monk and soldier, were responsible for most of Valletta's churches. Some of the best are described below; the greatest, St John's Co-Cathedral, is covered on pages 42–3.

CARMELITE CHURCH

The massive dome of the Carmelite Church, built to rival the nearby Anglican cathedral, is a dominant (and much-criticised) feature of the Valletta skyline. Originally built in 1573 by Gerolamo Cassar, after the devastation of World War II a new structure of far larger proportions was built around the old church. The interior is light, spacious and unusually free of elaborate ornamentation.
Triq it-Teatru il-Qadim (Old Theatre Street). Open: weekdays 6am–noon, 4–7.30pm. Free.

CHURCH OF GESÙ

Dating from the late 16th century, this ornate church was built in conjunction with the Jesuit College. When the Jesuits were thrown off the island in 1768, the college became the University of Malta and this is now its church. The interior is worth a visit for the paintings and carvings.
Triq il-Merkanti (Merchants' Street). Open: weekdays 5.45am–noon, 4–7.30pm; Sunday and public holidays 5.45am–noon only. Free.

CHURCH OF OUR LADY OF VICTORIES (La Vittoria)

This is the oldest building in Valletta, built to commemorate the Knights' victory in the Great Siege of 1565. Grand Master La Valette laid the foundation stone in 1566 and, according to his wishes, was buried in the church. His body was later moved to the crypt of the Co-Cathedral where many Grand Masters were subsequently buried. Our Lady of Victories was redesigned in baroque style in the 17th century and a bell tower was added in 1752. The two houses next to the church, distinguished by the fat mouldings on the windows and ceramics, are two of the very oldest houses in the city. The smaller one belonged to the priest.
Triq Nofs-in-Nhar (South Street). Closed for restoration much of the time. Free.

CHURCH OF ST PAUL'S SHIPWRECK

This is one of the oldest and most elaborate of the city's churches. The interior is richly endowed with coloured marble and a profusion of gilded woodwork. The vault is decorated with frescos depicting scenes from the life of St Paul. The church also possesses a finely carved wooden statue of St Paul which is carried through the streets of Valletta on 10 February, the Feast of St Paul. This is one of the island's main *festas*.
Triq San Pawl (St Paul's Street). Open: Monday to Saturday 11am–1pm, 4–6pm. Free.

GREEK CATHOLIC CHURCH

The church contains a 12th-century icon which is said to have been brought by the Knights from Rhodes in the 16th century.
Triq l-Arċisqof (Archbishop Street). Open: daily 7.30–10am; Sunday and public holidays 5–10am. Free.

ST PAUL'S ANGLICAN CATHEDRAL

Dowager Queen Adelaide, widow of Britain's King William IV, visited Malta during the winter of 1838–9, and was so appalled at the lack of an Anglican church in Valletta that she decided to pay for one to be built. The cathedral was built in classical style but with a not-incongruous Gothic spire which soars 65m above the city.

Pjazza Indipendenza (Independence Square). Open: Monday to Saturday 8am–noon. Free.

St Paul's Shipwreck Church

Grand Masters' Palace

*T*he 18th-century traveller, Patrick Brydone, noted that 'the Grand Master (who studies conveniency more than magnificence) is more comfortably and commodiously lodged than any prince in Europe, the King of Sardinia perhaps only excepted'. Despite malicious pillaging by Napoleon's troops following the French occupation in 1798 (and an inappropriately severe façade), the palace still gives you a good idea of the splendour to which the Grand Masters were accustomed.

Converted from a smaller house, the palace was designed by Gerolamo Cassar in 1571. From the time of its completion until the end of the Order's reign in Malta (1798), the palace was used by all the Grand Masters. In 1800 it became the official residence of the British governors. The palace is now the Presidential Office and Malta's Parliament House.

Armoury
Only about a quarter of the arms and armour belonging to the Knights has survived, but it is still a formidable

The outside of the Grand Masters' Palace betrays nothing of the splendour within

collection, with around 6,000 pieces in all. Among them are daggers, rapiers, halberds, cannons, pistols and some stunningly decorated suits of armour. In one room rows of Knights in armour stand to attention, while the special suits of armour individually made for the Grand Masters are displayed separately. The most splendid of these is the suit inlaid with gold made for Grand Master Wignacourt in 1610–20. Among the weapons and armoury of the Knights' adversaries are Turkish battle axes, helmets, gilded shields and a sword said to have belonged to the corsair, Dragut.

Courtyards
The two courtyards originally formed

one large area. Neptune's Court, in the centre, is named after a bronze statue of the sea god, standing among greenery, which is said to have been rescued from the old fish market in the 17th century. Prince Alfred's Court is smaller and more intimate, planted with palms, pittosporum and a charming jacaranda tree. On the elaborate clocktower four bronze figurines of Moorish slaves strike the hours.

State rooms

Short guided tours take place at regular intervals, provided that the State Rooms are not in use. Visits start in the Tapestry Chamber, originally the Council Chamber of the Knights. The walls here are hung with stunning Gobelin tapestries, featuring tropical scenes set in South America, the Caribbean, India and Africa. The tapestries, though nearly three centuries old, look as good as new, and were given to the Order by Grand Master Ramon Perellos in 1710.

Of all the rooms the most magnificent is the Hall of St Michael and St George, also known as the Throne Room, decorated with a cycle of 12 frescos, vividly portraying the 1565 Siege of Malta. The artist was Matteo Perez d'Aleccio, an engraver and painter who had once helped Michelangelo with the Sistine Chapel.

These highly detailed scenes start with the Fall of St Elmo on 23 June 1565 and end with the departure of the Turkish fleet from Malta on 8 September. Opposite the throne there is a charming gallery made from the stern of the great carrack, the *Santa Maria*, in which the Grand Master de l'Isle-Adam sailed away from the island of Rhodes in 1522, fleeing the forces of Suleiman the Magnificent.

The Hall of the Ambassadors was originally the Grand Master's audience chamber. Known also as the Red Room, this is decorated in crimson with Louis XV furniture and a high frieze recalling episodes from the early history of the Order when it still had bases in Jerusalem, Cyprus and Rhodes.

Leading off the Hall of St Michael and St George, the State Dining Room has magnificent 17th-century chandeliers and portraits of British monarchs, from King George III to Queen Elizabeth II. *Triq ir-Repubblika (Republic Street), overlooking Misrah il-Palazz (Palace Square). Tel: 221221. Standard opening hours (see page 185). Admission charge for Armoury and State Rooms.*

Gorgeous Gobelin tapestries depict the Indies as a tropical paradise

THE KNIGHTS OF ST JOHN

The Knights of the Order of St John of Jerusalem (to give their full name) were formed long before their reign on Malta. The Order was originally established in 1085 as a community of monks responsible for looking after the sick at the Hospital of St John in Jerusalem. They later became a military order, defending crusader territory in the Holy Lands and safeguarding the perilous routes taken by medieval pilgrims. The Knights were drawn exclusively from noble families and the Order acquired vast wealth from those it recruited and later from the ill-gotten gains of their privateering.

The Knights came to Malta in 1530, having been ejected from their earlier home on Rhodes by the Turks in 1522. Charles V, the Holy Roman Emperor, gave them the choice of Malta or Tripoli as a new base. Neither was to their liking, but nothing, they thought, could be worse than Tripoli.

Having chosen Malta, the Knights stayed for 268 years, transforming what they called 'merely a rock of soft sandstone' into a flourishing island with mighty defences and a capital city coveted by the great powers of Europe.

The Order was ruled by a Grand Master who was answerable only to the Pope. Knights were chosen from the aristocratic families of France, Italy, Spain, England and Portugal. On acceptance into the Order they were sworn to celibacy, poverty and obedience. Few lived up to these ideals; many were very wealthy and the Knights' standoffish attitude towards the locals does not always seem to have applied when it came to temptations of the flesh.

Ironically, it was the two great victories of the Knights which spelt the death-knell of the Order. The Great Siege of 1565, followed by the crucial Battle of Lepanto in 1571, were so successful in checking the Ottoman

Soldiers and priests, the Knights were once drawn from Europe's noblest families

advance into the western Mediterranean, that there was no longer an Infidel to fight. The Order gradually grew complacent and corrupt, with little to do but scour the seas for any booty that could be seized from Muslim ships.

By the late 18th century the Order was little more than a large but effete international gentlemen's club. The island was ripe for picking by Napoleon in 1798. When, four years later, the Order was formally restored to Malta, the Maltese resisted their return and instead sought the protection of the British.

Below: Attention! Armour in the Palace of the Grand Masters

MALTA EXPERIENCE

Appropriately located in the converted Hospital of the Order of St John, this multivision show highlights over 5,000 years of Malta's history – from neolithic origins to modern-day tourism. Some 3,000 colour slides, high-tech sound effects and a lively commentary combine to make this an easy, entertaining way of acquiring a basic knowledge of Malta's complex past. The commentary is available in eight languages.

The entrance is at the bottom of Triq il-Merkanti (Merchants' Street), across the road from the Mediterranean Conference Centre. Tel: 243776. Shows lasting 40 minutes from Monday to Friday every hour from 11am to 4pm, Saturday and Sunday at 11am and noon. Admission charge.

MALTA GEORGE CROSS – THE WARTIME EXPERIENCE

This 45-minute audio-visual show combines stills, movies and sensurround sound systems to tell the story of the Siege of 1942. The show was opened in 1992 to commemorate the 50th anniversary of the awarding of the George Cross to Malta.

Hostel de Verdelin, Misrah il-Palazz (Palace Square). Tel: 247891. Shows from Monday to Friday every hour from 10am to 4pm, Saturday 10am, 11am and noon. Admission charge.

MANOEL THEATRE

This gem of a theatre is said to be the third oldest in Europe. It was built in 1731 by the Portuguese Grand Master, Manoel de Vilhena 'for the honest entertainment of the people'. The

The Manoel Theatre, restored to its former glory

religious life to which the Knights were committed did not stop them indulging in theatrical pursuits. Watching or participating in pageants, operas, comedies and tragedies was very much part of their lifestyle.

The Manoel has had a chequered history and, after a flourishing beginning, it was variously used as a doss house, dance hall and cinema. During the 1860s, thanks to the enlarged garrison and fleet and an increase in the number of visitors to Malta, the theatre was declared inadequate and sold to finance the building of the new Royal Opera House in Valletta. It was not until the Opera House was laid to ruins in World War II that the Manoel came to life again. In response to a public appeal the Maltese government acquired the building and experts from Britain and Italy were called in to supervise its restoration. The glorious ceiling, with its gilding of 22-carat gold, and the tiny *paysages* (rural scenes) decorating the boxes were all restored to their original splendour. In December 1960 the grand reopening was celebrated by the Ballet Rambert's performance of *Coppelia*. Since then the theatre has never looked back. The Bonici Palace adjoining the theatre has also been restored to form the theatre foyer. Decorated with Viennese chandeliers, antiques from the *auberges* and engravings of theatrical scenes, this is now a venue for chamber-music concerts, lectures and art exhibitions. *Triq it-Teatru il-Qadim (Old Theatre Street). Guided tours Monday to Friday 10.30am and 11am. Tel: 246389. Admission charge.*

NATIONAL LIBRARY

Also known as the Biblioteca, this is an imposing arcaded building of the late

Malta's National Library houses a large collection of rare documents

18th century. The original library was built by the Knights in 1555. From 1612, the sale of any book belonging to deceased Knights was forbidden, hence this vast collection of valuable leather-bound tomes. Among the documents to be seen here is a letter in which Henry VIII proclaims himself head of the Church of England. Equally interesting are some of the 17th- and 18th-century books written on Malta by British visitors.

Misrah ir-Repubblika (Republic Square). Tel: 224338. Open: 16 June to 30 September, Monday, Tuesday, Thursday and Friday 8.15am–1.15pm; 1 October to 15 June, Monday, Tuesday, Thursday and Friday 8.15am–1pm and 1.45–5.45pm, Saturday 8.15am–1.15pm. Closed: Wednesday, Sunday and holidays. Free.

The ample torso of the female statuette known as the 'Venus of Malta'

NATIONAL MUSEUM OF ARCHAEOLOGY

For anyone remotely interested in prehistory, this rich repository of Malta's archaeological treasures is essential viewing. If you have already seen Malta's temples and tombs, the museum will be doubly rewarding because it contains many archaeological finds taken from those sites to prevent erosion. If you have not seen them yet, a tour of the museum should fire your enthusiasm to visit at least the major prehistoric sites of Malta.

Exhibits aside, the museum has the privilege of occupying the only *auberge* open to the public. One of the more luxurious of its kind, the Auberge de Provence was designed in 1571 by Gerolamo Cassar for the Knights of the *langue* of Provence (see page 29).

The most remarkable finds are those on the ground floor, covering the Bronze and Iron Age and the Temple and Neolithic periods. Exhibits are well displayed behind glass cabinets with excellent English labelling and fascinating small scale reconstructions of the temple complexes. Among the finds are flints, pottery, human skulls, necklaces and remarkably modern-looking obese female statuettes.

Among the highlights are discoveries from the Hypogeum underground burial site, such as the obese and headless *Venus of Malta* and the *Sleeping Priestess*, also endowed with ample features. The Tarxien section contains a wealth of treasures from the Tarxien temples, including pots and vases (which have been painstakingly reassembled), carbonised seeds and grasses found in cinerary urns, and the lower half of the famous fat fertility goddess. You can also see decorative blocks, removed from the temples and replaced by replicas, ornamented with elaborate spiral motifs and dating from 3000–2500BC.

Two upstairs rooms, devoted to Roman, Punic and Phoenician exhibits, are closed indefinitely for restoration. *Auberge de Provence, Triq ir-Repubblika (Republic Street). Tel: 235254. Standard opening hours (see page 185). Admission charge.*

NATIONAL MUSEUM OF FINE ARTS

This art collection occupies three floors of a fine baroque *palazzo*, built by the

Knights in the 16th century and remodelled in the 18th century. For many years it served as the official residence of the Commander-in-Chief of the British fleet and was commonly known as Admiralty House.

The collection begins with medieval Italian works and goes through to modern Maltese art. The highlights are the baroque paintings by Mattia Preti and the 20th-century sculpture by Antonio Sciortino.

Visits start on the first floor, reached via a splendid rococo staircase. Plaster-casts by the Maltese sculptor, Antonio Sciortino (1879–1947), are well displayed. The sculptor was obsessed with the theme of dynamic movement – illustrated well by the cast of *Speed*. Room 8 features a painting of *Christ the Redeemer* by Guido Reni which once hung in the private suite of the Grand Masters' Palace. Rooms 8 to 11 have a series of large and striking canvases in the style of Caravaggio.

Room 12 is devoted to the work of Mattia Preti (1613–99) who transformed St John's Co-Cathedral into a blazing monument to the glory of the Order (see pages 42–3). Preti came from Calabria but moved to Malta in 1661 to decorate the cathedral. He was made a Knight and spent the last 40 years of his life here. His paintings, full of movement and scenic effects, demonstrate the strong influence of Caravaggio and – in their colouring – Venetian artists of the late 16th century.

The ground floor rooms are devoted to 18th-century French and Italian painters, plus a section on modern Maltese art. Antoine de Favray's *The Visit* illustrates a typical bourgeois Maltese interior of the 18th century and the views of Valletta by Louis du Cros give a good idea of what the city looked like two centuries ago.

The basement contains *memorabilia* of the Order, including portraits of dignitaries, ceramics and silverware from the Sacra Infirmeria (see page 41). *Triq Nofs-in-Nhar (South Street). Tel: 225769. Standard opening hours (see page 185). Admission charge.*

The National Museum of Fine Arts is housed in the former Admiralty building

Assorted items of military hardware in the War Museum in Fort St Elmo

THE GEORGE CROSS

The George Cross was instituted by King George VI 'for acts of the greatest heroism or of the most conspicuous courage in circumstances of extreme danger'. Malta is the only nation to have been awarded the medal. The award of the medal is explained in a letter of 15 April 1942 sent from Buckingham Palace to the Governor of Malta:

'To honour her brave people I award the George Cross to the Island Fortress of Malta to bear witness to a heroism and devotion that will long be famous in history.'

To commemorate the 50th anniversary of the award Queen Elizabeth II and the Duke of Edinburgh visited Malta in 1992.

NATIONAL WAR MUSEUM

Fort St Elmo is famous for its role in the epic Siege of 1565 and, more recently, for its role in World War II; it thus makes a fitting home for Malta's National War Museum. The war relics shown here date from 1798, but the main emphasis is on World War II.

The chief exhibits are displayed in the main hall: an Italian E-boat, flanked by two World War I German torpedoes, Italian and German anti-tank guns and the aircraft *Faith* – sole survivor of Malta's tiny air force, made up of just three Gloster Gladiators (*Faith, Hope* and *Charity*). Set in an alcove is the George Cross awarded to Malta by King George VI on 15 April 1942.

Photographs taken during World

War II serve as a chilling reminder of the devastation caused to Malta by German bombardments and of the dire conditions suffered by servicemen and civilians. Among the other exhibits are wrecked aircraft raised from the seabed, relics of the destroyers sunk in Grand Harbour, a replica of an air-raid shelter and displays of battledress and gas masks.

Fort St Elmo. Tel: 222430. Standard opening hours (see page 185). Admission charge.

SACRA INFIRMERIA
(Holy Infirmary)

Wherever the Knights set up a base they built a hospital, and Malta was no exception. The Sacra Infirmeria, begun in 1574, had the longest hospital ward in the world (155m) and acquired international fame for its equipment and high medical standards. In the 17th century it was described as having 'one of the grandest interiors in the world'. Patients were fed from silver plates and were looked after by novices, by the Knights and sometimes even by the Grand Master himself.

The Order was obliged to take in the sick, the destitute and the insane regardless of their religion. Protestants, Muslims and members of the Greek Orthodox church were, however, put in a separate ward. For many years the only privilege a sick Knight could claim was two sheets instead of one. However, by the 17th century, many members of the Order had their own rooms, and they were soon to be the only patients allowed to eat off silver platters.

When the Order was ousted from Malta, Napoleon threw out the patients, looted the silver and melted it down to pay the troops who had taken part in his Egyptian campaign.

Under British rule, the Sacra Infirmeria became a military hospital and part was used as stables. The building was badly damaged during World War II though this did not stop it being used by the troops for social occasions. It was years before the government took steps to restore the building. The grand reopening, this time as a conference centre, took place in 1979. The expert restoration, blending old with new, won it the Europa Nostra Award. Tragically, the main hall was destroyed by fire in 1987 but it has now been rebuilt. Below the building, in a modern auditorium, you can see the Malta Experience (see page 36).

Triq il-Mediterran (Mediterranean Street). Tel: 243840. The conference centre is open to the public when the halls are not in use. Ask for permission at the entrance. Free.

Doorway into the old part of the Knights' Sacra Infirmeria

St John's Co-Cathedral

*T*he simple, sober façade of St John's gives no hint of its lavish interior. It was built as the conventual church of the Order and the Knights spent enormous sums of money embellishing the chapels of their *langues*. Almost every last piece of the walls, vault and chapels is painted, gilded or carved. Knights and Grand Masters are omnipresent in the form of their heraldic arms, monuments and mausoleums. The *pavimento* (floor paving) consists of numerous multi-coloured marble tombstones, bearing – along with carvings of skeletons and symbols of death – the names and escutcheons of past members of the Order.

The cathedral was built between 1572 and 1581 by Gerolamo Cassar and his training as a military engineer accounts for the sober exterior. Nearly a century later the prolific Italian artist, Mattia Preti, transformed Cassar's severe interior into a glowing showpiece of baroque art. His greatest task, which occupied him for five years, was the decoration of the vault. This he enriched with a narrative cycle depicting the life of St John the Baptist, painting with oils straight on to stone.

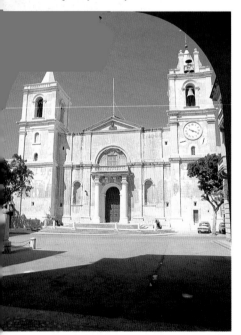

The measured façade of the Co-Cathedral, designed by a military architect

Chapels

Each of the side chapels belonged to the *langues*. They are variously decorated, but characteristic features are the symbols of the individual *langues* and the arms of the various Grand Masters. Preti's paintings decorate many of the chapels; worth singling out are *St George and the Dragon* in the Chapel of Aragon, Catalonia and Navarre (fourth bay on the right) and the serene *Mystical Marriage of St Catherine* in the Chapel of Italy (ninth bay going round). This latter chapel also contains Caravaggio's painting of *St Jerome*. The monuments to the Grand Masters are works of art in their own right, the very finest being the richly decorated marble and bronze mausoleums to Grand Masters Nicolas Cotoner and Ramon Perellos in the Chapel of Aragon, Catalonia and Navarre.

Crypt of the Grand Masters

The remains of 12 Grand Masters are buried here, mostly in sarcophagi. The only ordinary Knight buried in the crypt is Sir Oliver Starkey, English secretary to Grand Master La Valette during the Great Siege.

Museum and oratory

Of all the artistic treasures in the church, the *pièce-de-résistance* is generally considered to be Caravaggio's painting of *The Beheading of St John*. This huge, vigorous work of art dominates the oratory.

The highlights of the museum are the splendid Belgian tapestries based on paintings by Poussin and Rubens. During June, the month of the *festa* of St John, the tapestries are brought out of the museum to adorn the church interior.

Pjazza San Gwann (St John's Square). Tel: 225639. Open: Monday to Friday 9.30am–1pm, 1.30–4.30pm; Saturday 9.30am–1pm. Museum open: Monday to Friday 9.30am–1pm, 1.30–4.30pm. Crypt open: on request. Admission charge to museum only.

Inside, the Co-Cathedral is resplendent with tapestries and wall paintings

CARAVAGGIO

Michelangelo Merisi was known as Caravaggio, after the town near Milan where he was born in 1573. One of the most revolutionary painters of his day, he founded a school of painting based on realism heightened by the dramatic use of *chiaroscuro* (light and shade).

Caravaggio was notorious for his violent temper. His career in Rome came to a sudden end when he stabbed a man during a game of racquets and was forced to flee to Naples. In 1608 he came to Malta and painted a portrait of Grand Master Wignacourt. As a reward he was made a Knight of the Order and commissioned to paint the two works which can still be seen in St John's Co-Cathedral. However, his temper flared up again and an attack on one of the most senior Knights led to his imprisonment. He made a dramatic escape and fled to Syracuse, but in 1610 he died of a fever at Porto Ercole on the Tuscan coast.

Valletta Harbour Cruise

Taking a cruise around Malta's two great harbours will give you a fascinating insight into the island's long history. The cruiser weaves in and out of every creek, providing views of Valletta's bastions, forts and docks. You will also see numerous boats, ranging from monster cruisers and ocean-going tankers to tiny, brightly painted fishing boats.

The cruiser heads south across Sliema Creek; the dome of the Carmelite church and the spire of St Paul's Anglican Cathedral dominate the Valletta skyline.

1 MANOEL ISLAND

As the boat rounds Manoel Island, the semi-derelict and overgrown Fort Manoel comes into view. This was built in 1726 by the French as a garrison for 500 men. On the south side of the island, the Lazzaretto San Rocco, built by the Knights to house victims of the plague, leprosy and other infectious diseases, stands abandoned on the shore. *The boat skirts Lazzaretto Creek which, with Msida Creek, is Malta's major yachting marina. It then rounds the promontory of Ta'Xbiex, where several embassies occupy large mansions, before entering Msida Creek.*

2 THE *BLACK PEARL*

At the head of Msida Creek the *Black Pearl* was a Swedish brigantine which caught fire in the Suez Canal and was abandoned in Marsamxett Harbour. She was brought to life again for use in the film *Popeye*, shot at Anchor Bay in Malta (see page 111). More recently she has been used as a restaurant.

Next stop Valletta

Cruising across to Pietà Creek, the boat passes Gwardamanġa Hill, where Princess Elizabeth (later Queen Elizabeth II) stayed as a guest of Lord Mountbatten when Prince Philip was stationed in Malta. From here the boat plies across the harbour towards the open sea, skirting the great fortifications of Floriana and Valletta.

Weather permitting, Captain Morgan Boats (tel: 331961) depart six times a day from the Strand in Sliema. The tour, with commentary, lasts 70 minutes.

3 GRAND HARBOUR

This great natural harbour, with its sheltered anchorages and creeks, has been coveted by many a foreign fleet. Fort St Elmo, to the right, and Ricasoli Fort, to the left, guard both sides of the harbour entrance.

As you cruise along the eastern side of Valletta, look out for the main landmarks (described in more detail on pages 48–9). After Fort St Elmo, you will see the Memorial Siege bell, followed by the Lower and Upper Barracca Gardens. Skirting the eastern defences of Floriana, the cruiser then heads into Marsa Creek which, with its monster cranes, huge tankers, its shipyard and power station, is the most industrialised part of the harbour. *From here the boat turns round to explore the creeks and dockyards of the Three Cities on the opposite side of the harbour.*

4 DOCKYARDS AND CREEKS

The Knights established the first dockyard here in Malta's Grand Harbour. The dry docks date back to 1804. By 1938 the number of dockyard workers here reached 12,000; today the number is around 5,000, mostly employed in ship-repair work. French Creek, the next inlet, affords good views of repair docks and the tightly packed flat-topped houses of Senglea, where many of the workers live.

Rounding the tip of Senglea peninsula, where a stone *vedette* (lookout post) carved with an eye and an ear keeps watch over the harbour, the boat enters Dockyard Creek. Fort St Angelo occupies the tip of the next promontory. During the Siege the Knights strung a chain from the base of the fort to the shore of Senglea to keep out the Turks. Further into Dockyard Creek the large twin-belfried church of St Lawrence overlooks the waterfront.

Between the next two inlets, Kalkara and Rinella Creeks, you will see a graceful classical building, formerly a hospital. The boat exits the harbour past the semi-derelict Ricasoli Fort – once the biggest fort anywhere in the British Commonwealth – and returns to Sliema via St Elmo and the Tignè peninsula.

The scale of Malta's dockyards is only revealed when viewed from the air

Valletta

This stroll takes you through the heart of the city, past churches, palaces, *auberges* and a lot of modern shopfronts. Avoid Saturday afternoon and Sunday when the streets lack their characteristic bustle. *Allow 1 hour.*

Start at City Gate.

1 ROYAL OPERA HOUSE

From City Gate you enter Freedom Square where you will see the sad ruins of the Royal Opera House, once a splendid venue for theatre and opera. No attempt has been made to reverse the devastation of World War II, and opera performances now take place in the Manoel Theatre (see pages 36–7).

2 TRIQ IR-REPUBBLIKA (Republic Street)

Straight ahead of you is Republic Street, the city's main artery,

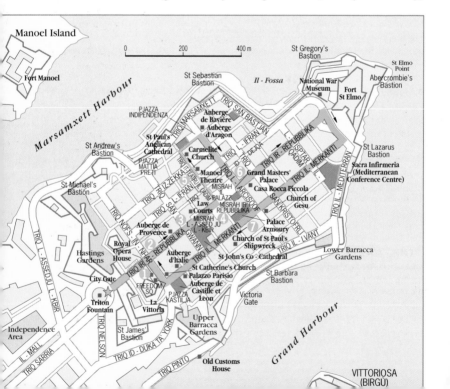

bustling by day with workers, shoppers and tourists, and in the evening with locals out for the *passiġġata* (promenade). A short way down on the left (just beyond the Air Malta offices at no 285) the Auberge de Provence houses the Museum of Archaeology (see page 38). *The next right turn takes you to the main entrance of St John's Co-Cathedral (see pages 42–3). If you divert here, return to Republic Street, turning right for Great Siege Square.*

3 MISRAH L-ASSED JU L-KBIR (Great Siege Square)

The allegorical monument, commemorating those who died in the Great Siege of 1565, is by the Maltese sculptor, Antonio Sciortino (1879–1947). Near by the horsedrawn *karrozzin* wait patiently for customers. Across the road the Law Courts occupy an imposing modern building in classical style.

4 MISRAH IR-REPUBBLIKA (Republic Square)

A few steps further on will bring you to the tree-lined Republic Square. Stop here for coffee, either *al fresco* or in the pretty rococo salon of the Café Cordina. A statue of Queen Victoria sits in the square.

Immediately after the square turn left down Triq it-Teatru il-Qadim (Old Theatre Street) which slopes down to the harbour. Stop at the first street.

5 TRIQ ID-DEJQA (Strait Street)

The exceptionally narrow Strait Street was the only place where the Knights were allowed to fight duels. Once a notorious red-light area, known to British servicemen as 'The Gut', this is still fairly sleazy at night.

Walk to the end of the street, passing the Manoel Theatre (see pages 36–7), the Carmelite Church (see page 30) and various little groceries and bars. Note the plaque on the left to Sir Walter Scott who stayed in the building when it was a hotel. Turn right for Pjazza Indipendenza (Independence Square), overlooked by St Paul's Anglican Cathedral (see page 31), then return to Republic Street via Triq l'Arċisqof (Archbishop's Street), noting the variety of wooden and wrought-iron balconies. At Misrah il Palazz (Palace Square), overlooked by the Grand Masters' Palace (see pages 32–3), turn left down towards the steepest part of Republic Street.

6 CASA ROCCA PICCOLA

The small *palazzo* at no 74 provides a rare opportunity to visit a historic home still occupied by a Maltese noble family (open: daily 9am–1pm; tel: 231796; admission charge).
Walk down to Fort St Elmo, then turn right, then right again for Merchants' Street.

7 TRIQ IL-MERKANTI (Merchants' Street)

Running parallel to Republic Street, Merchants' Street is lined with small neighbourhood stores and tailors, as well as baroque churches and *palazzi*. The stalls of the food market and of the morning market provide a bustling scene.

Nearing the end of the street, note the Auberge d'Italie, now the General Post Office (see page 29), on the right and St Catherine's Church alongside. Opposite, the austere Palazzo Parisio was Napoleon's headquarters when he stayed on Malta in 1798.
A right turn at the end of the street, passing La Vittoria church on your left (see page 30), will bring you back to the start of Republic Street.

Valletta's Ramparts

Sense the excitement of the past as you walk along the mighty Valletta ramparts and overlook the great harbour where famous battles were fought. The Knights' great defensive system of bastions, curtains and forts was one of history's most remarkable military architectural feats. *The round circuit takes about 2 hours, allowing for stops.* Alternatively you can pick up a *karrozzin* (horse-drawn carriage). Prices are steep for this quaint form of travel, but there is always room for bargaining.

Start at City Gate. A stairway on the left takes you up to Pope Pius V Street, above the ramparts. Turn right for Hastings Gardens.

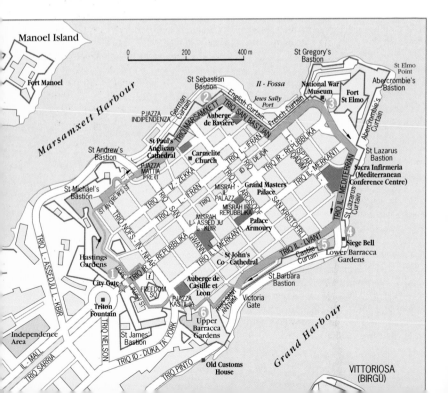

1 HASTINGS GARDENS

Forming part of the St John and St Michael Bastions, these gardens protect the rear of the city at the highest point of Mount Sceberras. Stop here for views of Floriana and, from the seaward end, Marsamxett Harbour.

Leaving the gardens bear right. Ahead you will see the lofty steeple of St Paul's Anglican Cathedral and the large dome of the Carmelite Church. Beyond St Andrew's Bastion, go down St Andrew's Street and further along, descend the Biagio steps. Carry on to St Sebastian Bastion.

2 ST SEBASTIAN BASTION

Stop for a drink here and admire the views across to Manoel Island, fortified by Grand Master de Vilhena between 1723 and 1732. Sliema's modern blocks rise behind.

Carry on along above the stalwart English and French Curtains, both named after the langues whose duty it was to defend them, to reach Fort St Elmo.

3 FORT ST ELMO

Occupying the vulnerable extremity of the Valletta promontory, this fort bore the brunt of the Turkish bombardments in the 1565 Siege (see pages 10–11). It was rebuilt after the siege and altered over the centuries. You can stop at the fort to see the National War Museum (see pages 40–1), but the rest of the interior is closed to the public.

On the far side of the fort, follow the ramparts along St Lazarus Bastion, from where there are panoramic views of the Grand Harbour. On the landward side the Sacra Infirmeria is now the Mediterranean Conference Centre (see page 41).

Make for the large bell overlooking the harbour.

4 SIEGE BELL OF MALTA

This 10-tonne bronze bell commemorates the 8,000 or so British and Maltese who fell in the 1940–3 Siege of Malta and was unveiled by Queen Elizabeth II and the President of Malta on 29 May 1992. Looking across Grand Harbour from here you can pick out the main landmarks of the Three Cities: to the left is the 17th-century Ricasoli Fort, and the former Bighi Hospital of Kalkara; at the tip of Vittoriosa's peninsula is Fort St Angelo, the oldest fort on the island and the principal stronghold of the Knights during the Siege.

Follow Triq il-Mediterran (Mediterranean Street) as it forks right, then turn left into the Lower Barracca Gardens.

5 LOWER BARRACCA GARDENS

There are splendid harbour views from the gardens and the temple commemorates Sir Alexander Ball, the British captain who assisted the Maltese in their uprising against the French in 1798.

Continue down Mediterranean Street to Triq il-Lvant (East Street) above the St Barbara Bastion. This joins Battery Street which will bring you up to Upper Barracca Gardens.

6 UPPER BARRACCA GARDENS

Once an exercise ground used by Italian Knights, these gardens command a spectacular panorama across the Grand Harbour to the Three Cities. The gardens also have a delightful statue by Sciortino of _Les Gavroches_ and various memorials to eminent British figures.

Turn inland to Pjazza Kastilja (Castille Place) overlooked by the Auberge de Castille et Léon. Cross to St James' Bastion, where the dry moat below is the scene of the Sunday morning market. The road marked 'Valletta Centre' will bring you back to your starting point above City Gate.

Valletta Environs

BIRKIRKARA

Part of the ever-spreading urban complex west of Valletta, Birkirkara has grown from an old town into a modern industrial suburb. The old centre, with its narrow streets and old residences, still has something of the look of a traditional Maltese village. The main interest lies in the churches. St Helena's is one of the island's biggest and richest churches, its spacious interior elaborately gilded and painted. The Church of the

The great and good of Malta are remembered in the Maglio Gardens

Annunciation built by Vittorio Cassar (son of the more famous Gerolamo) is an interesting example of Maltese Renaissance architecture, with more than a hint of Spanish in the façade. Newest of all is the sanctuary erected by the Carmelite Fathers on the edge of town.

Ħamrun

Ħamrun has some good shops, and is still known for basket-weaving. Otherwise the most interesting feature is the 17th-century aqueduct stretching between Ħamrun and Mdina. At Santa Venera, between Ħamrun and Birkirkara, the Casa Leoni (closed to the public) was built in 1730 for Grand Master de Vilhena, and stands in beautiful grounds.

Qormi

A busy manufacturing centre, Qormi was once known as *Casal Fornaro* (meaning the Village of Bakers). It still has a reputation for its bread, though the old baking methods are fast disappearing. The old quarter of narrow streets north of the town has some finely carved doorways and balconies. One of the earliest buildings is Stagno Palace (1589) in Dun Marigo Street, whose unusual façade has good examples of the typical Maltese 'fat' mouldings. The graceful Church of St George, at the eastern end of Qormi, was built at the end of the 16th century and retains its Renaissance façade.

FLORIANA

The suburb of Floriana was built in 1634 to extend the fortifications of Valletta in the event of renewed Turkish attacks. An Italian military engineer called Paolo

Floriani was responsible for the defences and so the suburb was named after him. Today it is a rather faded, aesthetically unexciting place, the most prominent features being the war memorials and the monuments to Maltese worthies. The streets are normally clogged with traffic, but the gardens are pleasantly spacious.

Maglio Gardens

This tree-lined walk through central Floriana was once a recreational ground where the Knights were supposed to work off their excess energy and thereby distract themselves from ideas of more lustful pursuits. Among the monuments is a statue of Grand Master de Vilhena which was taken from Republic Square, then known as Queen's Square, in Valletta to make way for Queen Victoria.

The large Independence Arena to the north, once the old military Parade Ground, is now used as a football pitch and sports ground. To one end of the gardens, the Argotti Botanical Gardens have exotic plants and some rare species of cactus.

Between Il-Mall (The Mall) and Triq il-Sarria (Sarria Street).

Porte des Bombes

Forming the entrance to Floriana, this ceremonial gateway was built between 1697 and 1720. In the 19th century the arch was doubled and the curtain walls cut away to enable traffic to pass on either side.

St Publius Church

This large twin-towered church was named after the Roman governor of the island who was converted by St Paul. It was built in the 18th century but has been remodelled and restored since. The circular slabs in St Publius Square cover

Above and below: textures of Malta – festive flags and fresh bread

the old underground granaries. Behind the church the Sarria Chapel has paintings by Mattia Preti.

Pjazza San Publiju (St Publius Square).
Open: early mornings and early evenings.
Free.

Sliema

Set on a headland between Marsamxett Harbour and the open sea, Sliema is Malta's number one tourist area. It is also the island's most densely populated town. A century ago this was a quiet area, with a few houses, the odd tower and a small chapel. Then wealthy Vallettans came and built their elegant art nouveau residences along the promenade. The introduction of the bus service in the 1920s accelerated development and Sliema became a fashionable address. Today it is the largest and the most expensive residential area in Malta.

With the rash of high-rise development now dwarfing what remains of old Sliema, the town could hardly be described as beautiful. Along Triq it-Torri (Tower Road) the few surviving old façades look distinctly forlorn. In some cases there is literally no more than a façade, waiting to be demolished and replaced by some faceless modern block.

On the plus side Sliema is a lively resort, with excellent facilities and location. Valletta lies just across the water, its dramatic skyline seen clearly from the Sliema Creek waterfront. The capital is easily reached by bus or ferry. Sliema is also the starting point for

Tower blocks line one side of Sliema Creek with views of Valletta opposite

cruises and is well placed for touring the island. Nowhere is more than 40 minutes away by bus.

There are no sandy beaches but the coastline shelves gently to the water and the smooth rocks and lidos on the north side afford good swimming. A promenade runs all the way to St Julian's Bay, passing gardens and playgrounds.

On the south side of the headland, the Strand is the livelier of the two promenades. Here you can watch cruisers steam across Sliema Creek or ferries plying to Valletta. A dual carriageway separates the promenade from a commercialised strip of souvenir shops, cafés and restaurants.

The shopping centre lies between the two main promenades, where the road cuts across the headland. The two steep streets here are lined with banks, travel agents and smart boutiques. The Tignè peninsula, jutting towards Valletta, is a quieter area, with good swimming and facilities on the Qui-si-Sana waterfront. Fort Tignè, one of Valletta's last defences, is now mainly given over to government housing, while the old circular tower has been turned into a bar.

The Gzira area of Sliema is primarily residential. A bridge links it to Manoel Island, home to the now-dilapidated Fort Manoel, the Royal Yacht Club and the Phoenician Glass Works. Courtesy boats

SLIEMA

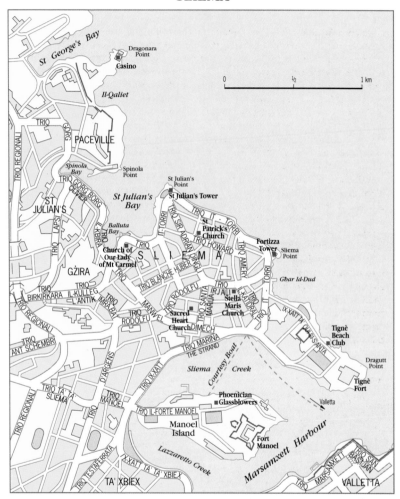

from Sliema will take you across to see the glass-blowing and the glasswork for sale. *Phoenician Glassblowers, Manoel Island. Tel: 313606. Studios open: Monday to Friday 9am–4pm, Saturday 9am–noon. Free.*

Sliema lies northwest of Vallettta, across Marsamxett Harbour. Ferries to the capital leave roughly every half hour, weather permitting. Buses 62, 63 and 67 go every 10 minutes.

Fashionable St Julian's is the place to eat out or dance the night away

ST JULIAN'S

From a simple fishing village, St Julian's has grown into a busy resort, sought after for its restaurants, bars and nightlife. Spinola Bay, surrounded by waterside cafés and restaurants, retains its brightly painted fishing boats though these days fishing activities are increasingly dwarfed by tourism. Evenings begin here with a drink or a meal (anything from a Chinese take-away to French *haute cuisine*); then, as the night draws on, the general drift is towards the discos of Paceville.

Balluta Bay, on the Sliema side, lacks the colour of Spinola Bay, but has pleasant palm-lined gardens by the water's edge and a water polo pool where the local team (one of the best in Malta) excites the crowds on Saturday evenings in summer.

St Julian's most blatant concession to tourism is the Paceville area, north of St Julian's Bay, where anonymous blocks of hotels and apartments, together with video bars, pubs and fast-food outlets, have sprouted with amazing rapidity. The dense concentration of discos and late-night bars make this the most popular area of Malta at night for the younger generation.

The Hilton International and Sheraton Dragonara Palace hotels, among the first developments of the area, take up most of the rocky shoreline. On Dragonara Point the casino occupies an elegant 19th-century mansion which belonged to Sir Hannibal Scicluna, founder of the first Maltese Bank.

On its north side Paceville merges with St Andrew's, once a large base for British military forces. The elegantly arcaded barracks are still very much in evidence, some turned into schools, others used for government housing.

The latest area of development is St George's Bay, which has a tiny but sandy beach with shallow sheltered waters. New construction includes a 600-bed 5-star hotel due for completion in 1995.

THE THREE CITIES

When the Knights of St John acquired Malta they chose to settle in the area known as *Il Borgo del Castello*, which later became Birgù. The only alternative would have been to settle in the medieval city of Mdina, but this might have aroused the hostility of the Maltese nobility who were already deeply ensconced there. In any case, Birgù offered a safe anchorage for the Knights' galleys. Thus they chose this long peninsula on which to build their first *auberges* and *palazzi*.

It was after the epic Siege of 1565 that Grand Master La Valette decided to give Birgù the new name of Vittoriosa (the

'Victorious'). To the locals, however, it is still, and always will be, Birgù.

Vittoriosa is the most interesting of the so-called 'Three Cities' – the other two being Senglea and Cospicua. The name 'cities' is somewhat misleading. The long thin peninsula which forms Vittoriosa is only 1km long, and the population is 3,540. In feel it is more like a small town than a city. Senglea, similarly, is spread out on a long thin peninsula, separated from Vittoriosa by Dockyard Creek. Cospicua links the two, its stalwart ring of forts protecting the cities on the landward side.

Cospicua (formerly called Bormla) was renamed after its ('Conspicuous') role during the Siege. Just to confuse things further, the city of Senglea was originally called L'Isla; it was renamed Invitta (the 'Unconquered') but this was changed to Senglea when it was fortified by Grand Master Claude de la Sèngle.

The dockyards in the area made an obvious target for German bombs during World War II. Most of Cospicua and Senglea was reduced to rubble, and the rebuilt suburbs are uninspiring. Saving graces are Cospicua's fortifications and Senglea's picturesque waterfront, while Vittoriosa has a charming centre.

COSPICUA (Bormla)

Building work began on the ring of bastions known as the Margherita Lines in 1639, but construction was interrupted by the decision to start the apparently more urgent Cotonera Lines. These massive fortifications, stretching for 4.5km, protected the cities on the landward side, though, like so many of the Knights' defences, they were never put to the test. The curtain walls are adorned with richly carved triumphal gateways, the finest of which is the Żabbar Gate on the Żabbar to Cospicua road (see page 104).

The elaborate Church of the Immaculate Conception (built in 1637) was one of the few buildings to survive the bomb attacks.

Cospicua's Church of the Immaculate Conception

The Three Cities lie across the Grand Harbour from Valletta. They can be reached by road, by water-taxi from the Old Customs House in Valletta or by bus from Valletta (for Cospicua nos 1, 2, 3, 4 and 6; for Senglea no 3; for Vittoriosa nos 1, 2, 4 and 6).

Senglea's waterfront promenade rises out of a sparkling blue sea

SENGLEA (L'Isla)

Another victim of World War II bombing, the best thing about Senglea today is the view from the waterfront. Here you can sit at an open-air café, watch the waterside activity and look across Dockyard Creek to Vittoriosa. The best vantage point for Valletta and the Grand Harbour is the Safe Haven Garden which replaced Fort St Michael in 1922. The original *vedette*, or lookout tower, with its symbolic sculptured eye and ear, still keeps watch over the harbour.

The ornate Church of Our Lady of Victories, almost entirely destroyed in the war, has since been completely restored.

VITTORIOSA (Birgù)

From 1530 until 1571, when the Order removed its seat to Valletta, Birgù was home of the Knights. Of all the Three Cities, it is the one that has altered the least. As the old capital, it has some imposing sites, including Fort St Angelo, the Church of St Lawrence, the Inquisitors' Palace and the *auberges* of

the Knights. You will find many tiny stores and shops, and narrow streets lined by ancient houses with beautiful stone balconies. The Maritime Museum and the Inquisitors' Palace are open to the public, but otherwise there are no real concessions to tourism.

Church of St Lawrence

The majestic baroque Church of St Lawrence has a fine setting overlooking Dockyard Creek. Built in the 16th century, this was the Knights' Conventual Church until St John's Co-Cathedral was built in Valletta.

The church was designed by the Maltese architect Lorenzo Gafà. Miraculously (given its proximity to the dockyards) the greater part of the church survived the bombing raids of World War II. Those parts that were damaged have been rebuilt and the dome has been redesigned on a larger scale.

Inside, the vault is decorated with paintings depicting episodes from the life of St Lawrence, and the finest work of art is Mattia Preti's large altarpiece on the same theme, *The Martyrdom of St*

Lawrence. There is also a huge and elaborate statue of St Lawrence which sees daylight once a year, on 10 August, when it is proudly paraded through the streets of Vittoriosa for the Saint's Day procession. Beside St Joseph's Oratory there is a museum containing treasures brought by the Knights from Rhodes. *Triq San Lawrenz (St Lawrence Street). Church open: Monday to Saturday 6–10am, 4–7pm. The museum has erratic opening hours. Free.*

THE THREE CITIES

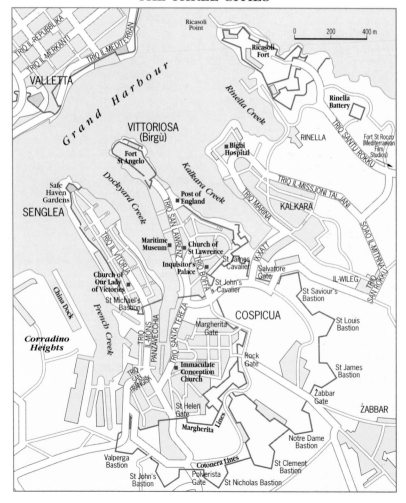

Fort St Angelo

On the tip of Vittoriosa, commanding the harbour, Fort St Angelo was the Knights' most impressive fortress. Believed to have been the site of a Phoenician, and later a Roman temple, it was fortified by the Arabs in the 9th century, then again by the Normans and the Aragonese in the 11th and 13th centuries. Between 1530 and 1576 it was the headquarters of the Order of St John and during the Great Siege it bore the brunt of the Turkish attacks after the fall of St Elmo. After 1576 it became the state prison of the Order. More recently the fortress was garrisoned by the British Army and from 1903 it became the headquarters of the Royal Navy.

The Inquisitors' rack is a grim reminder of the power of the Church

In the 1980s the fort was being used as a tourist complex, but since then the dance floor has been repaved, the swimming pool removed and much-needed restoration works are in hand. The fort is currently closed to the public, but the mighty walls are clearly visible from the bastions of Valletta.

Freedom Monument

In front of the Church of St Lawrence, the Freedom Monument, with a British sailor shaking hands with a local docker, commemorates the withdrawal of the British naval forces from Malta in 1979.

Inquisitors' Palace (Palazzo del Sant'Uffizio)

This palace is a grim reminder of the days of the Inquisition in Malta. Established in 1562 and abolished by the French in 1798, the Office of the Inquisition was set up to protect the Catholic faith and combat heresy. The official Inquisitor was often a powerful figure who abused his authority and became thoroughly unpopular with the Knights with whom he was supposed to co-operate. The palace, built in 1574, was used by the Inquisitors as their residence, court and prison.

The palace is now undergoing much-needed restoration. Rooms open to the public include the Court Room, the living quarters of the Inquisitors and the Main Hall whose ceiling is decorated with the Inquisitors' coats of arms carved in wood. In the dungeons you can still see graffiti scratched by the prisoners, many of whom went from here to the Court Room and thence to the execution yard.

Triq Boffa (Boffa Street). Tel: 827006. Standard opening hours (see page 185). Admission charge.

Perfect down to the last knot – model in the Maritime Museum

Maritime Museum

In 1842 the naval bakery was built over the site of the old slipway where the Knights used to repair their galleys and it remained a naval establishment until the British left Malta in 1979. In 1992 the bakery was converted into a maritime museum of Malta's remarkable seafaring heritage. Special sections are devoted to the navy of the Knights, the Royal Navy, fishing vessels, the merchant navy and traditional Maltese boats.

The Naval Bakery (on the waterfront). Tel: 805287. Standard opening hours (see page 185). Admission charge.

Post of England

This lookout point on the Kalkara Creek side of the Vittoriosa peninsula affords fine views of the seaward end of the Grand Harbour. From here you can see the neo-classical former Royal Naval Hospital, and, beyond it, the semi-derelict Ricasoli Fort.

MEDITERRANEAN FILM STUDIOS

On the coast north of Vittoriosa, close to Fort St Rocco, the Mediterranean Film Studios provide unusual facilities for international film-makers. Two cunningly sited water tanks face the sea to give the effect of a natural horizon as the backdrop. One is specifically designed for underwater shots; the other is a huge surface-shooting tank where ships of any size can be floated. The tank was used in *Christopher Columbus*, *Raise the Titanic*, the BBC's *Howards' Way* and many other major films and TV series.

Central Malta

*M*alta's central section, stretching from the Victoria Lines to the Valletta conurbation, is a region of gentle hills, terraced fields, farmsteads and a number of ever-expanding villages and towns.

The Victoria Lines, following the natural escarpment across the island, is a chain of British-built forts stretching from Madliena in the east to the great Bingemma Fort in the west. These were built to defend the most populated parts of the island from enemy landings in the west.

South of the Victoria Lines is Mdina, the jewel in Malta's Crown and a must for any visitor. The city's dynamic cathedral dome and the great walls of Malta's former capital rise above the plains of central Malta and command a huge sweep of the Maltese landscape. Just outside Mdina is the suburb of Rabat, best known for the labyrinth of catacombs beneath its streets. It is also a town of craftsmen, some of whom can be seen at work in the nearby village of

The ancient citadel of Mdina is one of Malta's highlights

Ta'Qali. Central Malta's other great cultural highlight is Mosta, whose colossal church dome is a conspicuous landmark from almost any vantage point in the area.

Although the region is essentially rocky and treeless, it contains two of the greenest spots on the island. Buskett Gardens is the only place on the Maltese archipelago where trees grow in profusion, while the gardens of the San Anton Palace have some of the most exotic flower and plant species to be found on any of the islands.

MDINA

It is hard to believe that the earthquake of 1693 destroyed the majority of Mdina's medieval and Sicilian-Norman buildings. Thanks to expert restoration, this gem of a city gives every impression of having survived all the ravages of time.

Crowning a hilltop at the centre of Malta, the magnificent cathedral dome and the walls surrounding the city can be seen from far away. Justifiably it is known as the 'Silent City'. Today's population is a mere 400, and most inhabitants appear to stay behind the tightly closed doors of their handsome town houses. It is rare that you ever have the chance to peep through an entrance into one of the lovely inner courtyards.

Only city residents are allowed to

MDINA AND RABAT

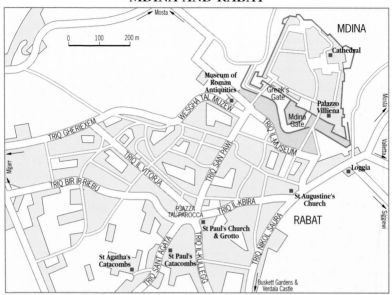

bring cars through the city gates (and commercial vehicles until 10.30am), and for most of the day the streets are peaceful. What is more, there is little sign of commerce. The only concessions to tourism are a handful of gift shops, a couple of inconspicuous restaurants and one guest house which occupies an old *palazzo*. The town is essentially one of peaceful alleys, handsome *palazzi*, old mansions and interesting museums. Nothing has been allowed to spoil its essentially medieval character. Even when large groups of tourists do descend on the city, it manages to retain a remarkably calm and dignified air.

Mdina is 10km west of Valletta. Bus 80 from Valletta.

Mdina is a city of peaceful alleys, fine churches and gracious old mansions

Mdina's architecture varies from medieval to more recent neo-Gothic

Architecture

Mdina is one of the few great architectural treats on Malta that did not result from the activities of the Knights of St John. Originally built by the Romans as the suburb to Rabat, the city was then named *Melita*. Under the Arabs it was reduced to its present size, refortified and given the name of Mdina. Rabat then became the suburb.

Under Aragonese rule, Mdina took on the medieval character that it preserves today and it was Alfonso V of Aragon who named it *Città Notabile* (Eminent City). Once the Knights built Valletta as the new capital, Mdina lost its worthy name and became simply the *Città Vecchia*, or Old City.

Mdina has always been the home of noble families and dignitaries. A famous former resident was Malta's first bishop, Publius, who was converted to

Christianity by St Paul; Malta's oldest titled family still resides in one of the palaces. Many of the residences were left empty for long periods when their owners moved to Valletta to join the Knights, but now almost all the old houses are lovingly maintained and any that are in disrepair are rapidly being restored.

The streets are narrow and winding, flanked by the mellow golden façades of baroque and restored medieval mansions. Many of them have fine stone or wrought-iron balconies and elaborate brass knockers on the doors. Despite the disparity in age between the medieval and the later baroque, the architecture, as a whole, is extraordinarily harmonious.

Most of the finest dwellings front on to Triq Villegaignon (Villegaignon Street), the city's major thoroughfare, which leads in a more or less straight line to the fortified northern edge of the city. From here there are wonderful views across the plains to Valletta. The alleys leading off Villegaignon Street were deliberately built narrow and angled to deflect the flight of arrows and shot. These silent alleys, off the beaten tourist track, are well worth exploring.

The Cathedral

The devastating earthquake of 1693 almost totally destroyed Mdina's old cathedral. The original church dated back to the 13th century and can be seen in two of Matteo Perez d'Aleccio's frescos in the Grand Masters' Palace in Valletta. Less than 10 years after its collapse, a new baroque church had risen in its place.

The cathedral was designed by the well-known Maltese architect, Lorenzo Gafà. By this time he had already designed several churches on Malta and was at the height of his career. The perfectly proportioned façade and the dynamic dome (by far his boldest and arguably the finest on Malta) make this the most impressive of all his churches. The work took just five years to complete and a number of houses were demolished at the same time to make way for a piazza appropriate to the size and splendour of the church.

Inside, the immediate impression is one of grandeur. Though not quite as rich as St John's Co-Cathedral in Valletta, it is nevertheless reminiscent of that church in the gilded carvings, the ornamental side chapels and the paintings that adorn the vault, apse and chapels. Many of the paintings and carvings illustrate scenes from the life of St Paul; the finest (but not the easiest to see) is Mattia Preti's mural of *The Shipwreck of St Paul*, decorating the apse. This was one of the few treasures in the old church which survived the earthquake.

As in Valletta's cathedral, the floor is inlaid with funerary slabs in multi-coloured marble commemorating bishops, prelates and various members of the Maltese aristocracy.
Pjazza San Pawl (St Paul's Square). Open: Monday to Saturday 9.30am–1pm, 1.30–3.45pm. Free.

The dizzying heights of the great cathedral dome viewed from within

Sturdy balconies and baroque enrichments abound in the streets around the cathedral

Cathedral Museum

Treasures salvaged from the original pre-earthquake cathedral are now housed in a splendid baroque palace which once served as a Diocesan seminary. The collection of paintings, prints, woodcuts and old master drawings is the legacy of Count Saverio Marchese (1757–1833), a wealthy patron of the arts. Particularly fine among the works of art are the woodcuts by Dürer, the engravings by Rembrandt and the 14th-century St Paul Polyptych which once adorned the high altar of the old cathedral. Here St Paul, enthroned in majesty, is surrounded by graphic depictions of episodes from his life. Among the other museum exhibits are finely illustrated choir books, elaborate vestments, silver plate and a coin collection spanning over 2,000 years, including a complete set of Roman coins minted on Malta and Gozo. The old refectory of the seminary has been preserved, as has the charming 18th-century octagonal chapel.

Pjazza Tal-Arċisqof (Archbishop's Square). Tel: 454697. Open: June to September, Monday to Saturday 9am–1pm and 1.30–5pm; October to May, 9am–1pm and 1.30–4.30pm. Admission charge.

Mdina Dungeons

The chambers, cells and secret underground passageways below the Palazzo Vilhena (Vilhena Palace) form the setting for Malta's most gruesome museum. Here the darker side of Malta's history is presented in a series of horrific waxwork scenes. Be prepared for gory scenes of torture and execution, dead rats, death-carts, heads on spikes and harlots and witches being whipped. Such scenes are a reminder that torture was only publicly and formally abolished in 1813 by Sir Thomas Maitland, British Governor of Malta.

Pjazza San Publiju (St Publius Square). Tel: 450267. Open: daily June to September, 10am–7pm; October to May, 10am–6pm. Admission charge.

Mdina Experience

This audio-visual show uses the latest in sound and light technology to take you through the tragedies and triumphs of the old capital. The auditorium occupies part of a well-converted 'Norman' house, which can also be admired while you take a drink at the bar.

7 Pjazza Mesquita (Mesquita Square). Tel: 454322. Open: Monday to Friday 11am–4pm, Saturday 11am–1pm. Admission charge.

Museum of Natural History

The magisterial Palazzo Vilhena is French in style and one of its finest features is the sculpted doorway, showing the coat of arms of Grand Master Manoel de Vilhena, who built it in the 18th century. The palace was later used as a temporary hospital during the outbreak of cholera in 1837, then as a military hospital for British troops from 1860.

Today the palace makes a fine setting for the Museum of Natural History. This is a pleasantly old-fashioned museum, with spacious rooms and excellent labelling in English. Different sections are devoted to minerals, fossils, fish, insects, mammals and birds.

Pjazza San Publiju (St Publius Square). Tel: 455951. Standard opening hours (see page 185). Admission charge.

Palazzo Falzon

This is one of the few opportunities you will have to see inside one of Mdina's aristocratic mansions. The so-called 'Norman House' was built in 1495 ('Norman' in Malta means anything from 1090, when the Normans arrived, to 1530, when the island was handed over to the Knights). This finely preserved mansion, with its graceful arched windows, is now a private museum whose rooms are decorated with paintings, antiques, weaponry and ceramics. The paintings and lithographs of Malta are particularly interesting for their portrayal of historical events on the island.

Triq Villegaignon (Villegaignon Street). Tel: 454512. Open: Monday to Friday 9am–1pm, 2–4.30pm. Admission charge.

The stately Palazzo Falzon is now a fascinating museum

St Paul's Church is built on the spot where the saint once preached

RABAT

Compared to the little medieval city of Mdina, silently enclosed within its walls, Rabat seems sprawling, bustling and very much alive. This is, after all, the commercial hub of central Malta. Unlike Mdina, Rabat has plenty of bars, shops and local life.

In Roman times Rabat and Mdina were one city. It was the Arabs who dug a ditch to isolate and protect Mdina, making Rabat the suburb. Today the town is visited for its churches, chapels, Roman remains and catacombs (see map on page 61).

Museum of Roman Antiquities/ Roman Villa

Although called the Roman Villa, this museum is actually housed in a neoclassical building, albeit on the site of a Roman town house whose original mosaic floor is an important exhibit. Other examples of mosaic work decorate the walks along with columns, capitals, statues and tombstones which have been unearthed in the area. Among the other finds are early-Christian oil lamps, Roman glass, Punic *amphorae* and ancient bronze fish hooks.

Wesgha Tal-Mużew (Museum Esplanade). Tel: 454125. Standard opening hours (see page 185). Admission charge.

St Paul's Church and the Grotto of St Paul

The parish church of Rabat, founded in 1575 but remodelled in 1692, was built over one of Malta's earliest Christian chapels. The Grotto of St Paul, below the adjoining Chapel of St Publius, is the main point of interest. According to the locals it was here that St Paul spent several weeks preaching Christianity; another story has it that the Apostle was imprisoned here. It is also said that stone scraped from the grotto walls has special healing powers and that, however much stone is scraped away, the cave never alters in size. The prominent feature, below a series of dimly lit catacombs, is a marble statue of St Paul.

The custodian will inform you that the grotto was once a Roman prison and will show you the holes in the roof from where the prisoners' chains once hung. Two tiny chapels are dedicated to St Paul and St Luke, each one with a statue of its apostle.

In 1990 Pope John Paul II visited Rabat and came to pray in the grotto. His parting prayer, 'God Bless Malta and the Maltese', is inscribed on a plaque on the exterior wall of the church.

Fascinating balconies feature on many older houses in Rabat

St Paul's Grotto, Pjazza Tal-Paroċċa (Parish Square). Open: daily 9.30am–noon, 2.30–4.30pm. No admission charge, but a tip to the custodian is welcomed. Entrance in the main square.

St Paul's Museum

This former clergy house, called Wignacourt College, is linked to St Paul's church by an underground passage. Lord Nelson came to visit the catacombs below in 1800 but these are no longer open to the public. In 1981 the college was converted to a museum and picture gallery where you can see Punic-Roman pottery, old maps, coins, books and furniture.

Triq il-Kulleġġ (College Street). Open: Monday to Saturday 9.30am–2.30pm. Closed in winter. Admission charge.

The Grotto of St Paul

RABAT'S CATACOMBS

Palestinian Jews first introduced the idea of burial in underground chambers. The Christians were quick to take up the idea, hewing tombs, canopies and tables out of the stone. The whole area beneath Rabat is honeycombed with such catacombs – over 3sq km of chambers have been discovered. Some can be visited, others are buried below later buildings and some are used as cellars.

St Agatha's Catacombs

The small church of St Agatha is dedicated to a young Sicilian saint who, according to local tradition, crossed to Malta to escape persecution during the reign of Emperor Decius (3rd century AD). The church's crypt is decorated with a fascinating series of Gothic and Renaissance frescos, depicting St Agatha and other saints. St Agatha's Catacombs lie below the church and you will be shown round by knowledgeable guides. There are pagan, Punic and Jewish burial chambers within this catacomb complex, but only the Christian section is open to the public. The dark narrow passageways are flanked by tombs of small groups or families, often with a circular stone table,

known as an *agape* table. It was here that ritualised funeral feasts took place to celebrate the anniversary of the death of relatives or friends. These tables were later replaced by altars. Remnants of ancient frescos are just visible on a few of the tomb walls.

In the convent alongside the church there is a museum displaying ancient pottery, statues, minerals and prehistoric animal remains, including a mummified alligator from the Nile (600–400BC).
Off Triq Sant'Agata (St Agatha's Street). Tel: 454504. Open: 16 June to 30 September, Monday to Friday 9am–5pm, Saturday 9am–4pm; 1 October to 15 June, Monday to Friday 9–11.45am and 1–3.45pm, Saturday 1–3.45pm, Sunday 9–11am. Guided tours only. Free.

St Paul's Catacombs

This is the largest of Rabat's catacomb complexes, an extraordinary labyrinth of narrow passages lined by rock-cut tombs. Like the catacombs of St Agatha, some of these have an *agape* table hewn out of the rock.
Triq Sant'Agata (St Agatha's Street). Tel: 454562. Standard opening hours (see page 185). Admission charge.

Rock-cut tombs in St Paul's Catacombs

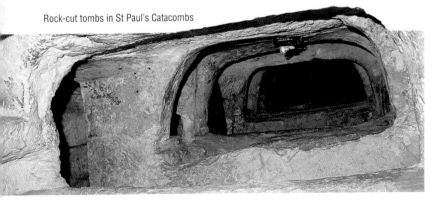

RABAT ENVIRONS
Buskett Gardens

In the heat of the summer, Buskett Gardens is a real oasis of greenery. The name is a corruption of the Italian *boschetto* meaning 'small wood' and there are certainly more trees than flowers. The paths are lined by pines and firs, cypresses and oaks, citrus and mulberry trees. The gardens are green all year though they are far more rewarding in spring than summer. The area is a public park, popular with both locals and visitors, especially at the end of June when it becomes the venue of the Imnarja (pronounced *ImNAHyah*) festival (see pages 72–3).

A focal point of the gardens is the long-established Buskett Roadhouse, where you can try Maltese cuisine and dance on summer evenings.
2.5km south of Rabat. Always open. Free. Bus route 82 between Valletta and Rabat.

Cart ruts at Clapham Junction

CART RUTS

The tracks that criss-cross several rocky plateaux on Malta and Gozo have puzzled archaeologists. Sometimes called 'the tramlines of neolithic man' they cut across the limestone in parallel lines, usually 1.35m apart. There are various theories as to their purpose but it is generally agreed they were made by, or created for, some sort of transportation system. They may have been formed by the constant use of animal-drawn sledges, or they may have been carved to guide a wheeled vehicle. Neither theory explains why some of the cart ruts, such as those at Clapham Junction, lead off the edge of the cliffs.

Clapham Junction

Clapham Junction is the name for the site of numerous prehistoric cart ruts – though to the uninitiated eye they are not immediately obvious. Look for the parallel and intersecting grooves carved in the limestone and running towards the cliffs.
Għajn il-Kbira (0.5km from Buskett Gardens). Always open. Free.

Dingli Cliffs

The highest village on Malta, Dingli lies on the west side of the island where the cliffs drop 253m to the sea. For those with a head for heights this remote and dramatic stretch of coast makes wonderful walking territory. It is particularly pretty in spring when tiny wild irises sprout from seemingly solid rock. Five kilometres offshore the steep rocky islet of Filfla rises up from the shimmering blue sea.

From the road skirting the clifftops the first impression you gain of the coastline is of a sheer drop to the sea. A glance over the clifftops reveals, at least 100m below, a wide shelf of neatly terraced and surprisingly fertile fields. Not so many years ago fishermen used to lower themselves from the terraces by

knotted rope, clinging to the rope with one hand and precariously casting out a line with the other.

The lonely Madalena Chapel perches on the coastline's highest point. This opens just once a year, for the feast of St Magdalene on 22 July. An inscription warns that the chapel cannot offer sanctuary from the law – a legacy of the 17th century when the Order of St John restricted the refuge offered by the church.

The only other real landmarks are a radar station and, along the aptly named Panoramic Road, a restaurant called Bobbyland which can provide a good rabbit stew and breathtaking views from the terrace on the clifftops.

Dingli Village

The village of Dingli lies just over 1km inland from the cliffs, the silver dome of its church dominating the skyline. The

Terraces tumble down the hillside in the area around Dingli Cliffs

road runs through a stony landscape irrigated by water drawn up from below ground by slim metal wind-driven pumps. Dingli is a small and unassuming village with a cluster of houses around the church and a handful of welcoming bars and cafés.

3km southwest of Rabat. Bus 81 from Valletta.

Verdala Palace

It is perhaps not surprising that Grand Master Hughes Loubenx de Verdalle, who was renowned for his love of pomp and splendour, chose one of the finest settings on the island for his summer retreat. The palace, set within its own park, overlooks the woods and citrus groves of the Buskett Gardens (see page 69).

The building was designed by Gerolamo Cassar in 1586 on the lines of a fortified castle. The moat surrounding the palace saw several suicides during Verdalle's reign. The Grand Master was notoriously cruel and to some of his servants drowning seemed preferable to the agonies of the torture chamber.

Today the palace is the official summer residence of the President and a showplace where VIPs are entertained. The finest room is the lofty banqueting hall, where a series of frescos depicts Verdalle's life and times, from his youth to his election as Grand Master and Cardinal. On the ceiling the figures from Greek mythology were painted over at the suggestion of Lady Bonham-Carter, wife of a British Governor who lived here. Happily these are gradually being restored.

A spiral staircase, which looks circular but is in fact elliptical, leads up to the first floor. The marble steps were purposely made shallow for the benefit of

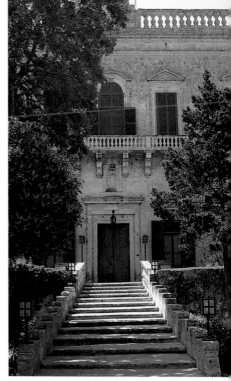

The elegant Verdala Palace was built as a cool and shady summer retreat

the Knights who had trouble bending their armour-plated knees.

The first-floor living quarters bear the mark of Grand Master Vilhena who succeeded Verdalle as Grand Master and elaborated on his palace. In the upstairs dining room the games boards chiselled into the stone floor were made by French officers who were imprisoned in the palace in 1812. The two bedrooms on this floor both have 'secret' staircases – one led down to the torture rooms, the other was an escape route for the Grand Master. Tours of the palace end on the rooftop with its panoramic views.

2.5km south of Rabat. Tel: 221221. Open: Tuesday and Friday only, 9am–noon and 2–5pm. Guided tours only. Free.

IMNARJA

If you happen to be on Malta at the end of June, head for the Buskett Gardens near Rabat (see page 69) where the island's most popular festival takes place. Traditionally known as the *Imnarja* (pronounced *ImNAHyah*), this is officially the Feast of St Peter and St Paul. It coincides with the end of harvest and is essentially a folk festival, where the crops are laid out on display and the crowds make merry with wine, food and song. The name *Imnarja* derives from the Italian word *luminària*, or illuminations, dating from the days when torches and bonfires lit up the ramparts of Mdina on the night of the *festa*.

The festival of Imnarja combines colour, pageantry and revelry with all the excitement of the horse racing that forms the climax of the whole occasion

On the weekend closest to St John's Day (24 June), the *festa* is heralded by a simple ceremony known as the *Bandù*. This takes the form of a procession to parade the *palji* (or banners) that will be given as prizes to the winners of the horse races that take place on 29 June.

On the eve of 28 June, the scene is set in the Buskett Gardens for a day and night of revelry. Vegetables, fruits, poultry, honey and wine are laid out for display, and vendors set up stalls selling *pastizzi* (cheese pastries), *mqaret* (date-filled pastries) and *qubbajt* (local nougat). Crowds then gather to cook the favourite Maltese dish of fried rabbit. Throughout the night bands play, guitarists strum and vast quantities of Maltese wine are consumed.

The following day sees the climax of the *festa*, celebrated with horse and donkey races held along Rabat's Racecourse Street. Traditionally the animals are ridden bareback, the jockeys spurring the animals on with a stick in either hand. At the end of the races the *palji* are handed out from a loggia at the foot of Saqqajja Hill. It was from here that the Grand Masters and other dignitaries used to survey the races. The winners take their *palji* which are then displayed in their parish church for the rest of the year.

ATTARD/THE THREE VILLAGES

The villages of Attard, Balzan and Lija have for many years been prosperous residential areas, typified by elegant residences and well-watered gardens, often hidden behind high walls. During the era of the Knights many affluent families moved away from crowded Valletta and set up their homes here. The villages have more or less merged into one and only the locals seem to know where the divisions lie.

ATTARD
San Anton Palace

'If living in lofty and splendid rooms be a pleasure, I have it.'
Samuel Taylor Coleridge, while staying in the San Anton Palace.

Enjoying the ducks and greenery in the gardens of the San Anton Palace

The French Grand Master Antoine de Paule (who took office in 1623) was notoriously vain and self-indulgent. The days of frugality within the Order were over, decadence had set in and de Paule was determined to lead a life of luxury. Considering the Verdala Palace too far from Valletta for his comfort, he chose instead to enlarge this country house near the village of Attard, turning it into the sumptuous Palace of San Anton. Here de Paule lived in great state along with his retinue of staff, including falconers, wig-makers, chefs, valets, domestic servants and a rat-catcher. To celebrate his first night in the palace, he gave a sumptuous banquet and invited all his staff and numerous VIPS.

In more recent history the palace served as the British Governor's residence. Today it is the private residence of the President. The palace is not open to the public but the gardens are.

San Anton Gardens

These luxuriant public gardens are laid out with avenues of trees, exotic shrubs and flowers, including species that you are unlikely to see anywhere else on the island. Apart from the cats that roam the gardens (many of them, sadly, abandoned by their owners), there is also a tiny zoo. *Gardens open: daily till sunset. Free.*

Church of St Mary

Attard's parish church is a remarkable achievement, built by Tommaso Dingli when he was only 22 years old. It was completed in 1613 and is one of the few noteworthy Renaissance buildings on Malta. The façade, reminiscent of a Roman temple, has a particularly fine carved doorway.

BALZAN AND LIJA

Desirable villas and a variety of churches are the notable features of these two villages. In Balzan the late 17th-century Church of the Annunciation in the main square has a baroque façade and more than a hint of Spanish influence in its design. The simple little Church of St Roch in Three Churches Street was built in 1593, and dedicated to the protector of plague victims.

In Lija the handsome church of St Saviour was built in 1694 by Giovanni Barbara. The essentially sober facade gives little hint of the elaborate frescoed interior. Lija has one of the island's most spectacular firework displays, held on the first Sunday after 6 August and celebrating the Feast of St Saviour.

The Three Villages lie about 6km west of Valletta. Bus 40 from Valletta (also bus 74 to Attard and Balzan).

A Palm Sunday cross decorates one of Gudja's older buildings

GUDJA

Since the construction of the neighbouring Luqa Airport, this farming village may have lost its identity, but it manages to preserve a handful of 17th- and 18th-century houses and four churches. The small Church of St Mary Ta'Bir Miftuh, on the outskirts, is one of the oldest churches on Malta, dating back to 1436. Gudja's main claim to fame is that it was the birthplace of the great Maltese architect, Gerolamo Cassar.

7km south of Valletta. Bus 8 from Valletta.

The monumental church of Mosta is crowned by one of Europe's biggest domes

LUQA

Luqa means poplar tree, a peaceful-sounding name that could hardly be less fitting for a village that now stands alongside Malta's airport. The location made it the inevitable target of air raids during World War II.

6km south of Valletta. Bus 32 from Valletta.

MOSTA

To most people the village of Mosta means the church of Mosta, or, more precisely, the massive dome. At the time of its completion in 1863 this was one of only a handful of church domes in Europe that came close to the biggest of them all, St Peter's in Rome. Throughout its construction, no internal supports were used – it was only with the help of mules and pulleys that the huge slabs were hauled up. The huge edifice was built around an older, much smaller church and it was here that services were held while construction work was in progress. The church took 27 years to build and once it was completed the old church was demolished.

The massive dome, totally out of proportion to the surrounding village, is visible from almost every vantage point in Malta. With its huge Ionic columns supporting the portico, the façade imitates the Pantheon in Rome. The church can hold around 10,000 people.

The most compelling exhibit in the museum is a replica of the World War II bomb which penetrated the dome and fell among the congregation. Photographs show the hole that was ripped in the roof.
8.5km west of Valletta. Tel: 433826. Open: Monday to Saturday 5am–noon, 3–8pm. Buses 53 and 57 among many others from Valletta.

MTARFA
The military buildings and hospital of Mtarfa lie on a ridge on the outskirts of Mdina, across the Wied il-Ħemsija (Ħemsija Valley). The barracks were set up by the British at the end of the 19th century and became derelict with the departure of the servicemen. In recent years they have been used as residences for Maltese families. The buildings and the clocktower can be clearly seen from Mdina's northern ramparts.
1km north of Mdina.

NAXXAR
Said to be one of the first villages to convert to Christianity after St Paul's arrival on the island, Naxxar is also one of the oldest villages in Malta. According to legend, St Paul preached in the chapel of San Pawl tat-Tarġa, just north of Naxxar. This small village is also known for its prehistoric cart tracks (see page 69).

Nowadays Naxxar merges with Mosta and is best known as the venue of the Malta International Trade Fair (1 to 15 July). This and other Maltese fairs and exhibitions are held in the grounds of the Palazzo Parisio. The parish church of Our Lady of Victory was built between 1616 and 1630.
8.5km west of Valletta. Buses 54 and 56 from Valletta.

SIĠĠIEWI
The predominant feature of this large farming village is the baroque church of St Nicholas. The crowning glory is the dome – one of the tallest in Malta. The church, which is lavishly embellished, was designed by Lorenzo Gafa in 1675, though part of the exterior dates from the 19th century. The huge piazza outside the church has always been the meeting place for the villagers. It is best seen on a Sunday morning, when locals gather dressed in their Sunday best.
6km southeast of Rabat. Bus 89 from Valletta.

The World War II bomb that ripped through Mosta's dome but did not explode

TA'QALI CRAFT CENTRE

The former World War II aerodrome at Ta'Qali is now the venue of the island's largest craft market. Although clearly aimed at the tourist market (it is one of the main stops on organised tours of the island), the prices here tend to be slightly cheaper than souvenir shops in resorts and towns. The wartime Nissen huts of the airbase make uninspiring showrooms but at least you can see all the Maltese handicrafts in one complex and you can watch the artisans at work: silversmiths fashioning filigree, craftsmen beating brass and iron, lacemakers creating shawls and tableware. The glass factory, on a limb from the rest of the complex, is perhaps the most impressive of the outlets, with a lovely range of vivid turquoise vases, glasses and decorative items. You can see the furnaces and watch the glass being blown before browsing in the air-conditioned shop. Prices are not high, especially if you choose from the range of 'seconds'.

For the Maltese, Ta'Qali's main draw is the national football stadium – venue for many international matches.

3.5km northeast of Rabat, well marked off the main Attard/Mdina road. Tel: 415786 (for information). Open: Monday to Friday

Making Maltese Crosses of polished marble in Ta'Qali Craft Centre

8am–5pm, Saturday 8am–12.30pm. Free. Bus no 65 goes direct from Sliema. Buses 80 and 81 from Valletta involve a 20-minute walk from the nearest bus stop to the Craft Centre.

VICTORIA LINES

Malta's great geological rift runs in a northeasterly direction from Ras ir-Raħeb, on the west coast, almost as far as Bahar iċ-Ċaghaq, on the east side of the island. This provided a natural defence for the British at the end of the 19th century. A line of detached forts, with supporting bastions, was constructed along the ridge, cutting off the shallow bays of the west which potentially provided easy landing for invaders.

Parts of the forts and bastions making up the lines can still be seen – either travelling by car along minor roads or along footpaths which command some magnificent views. One of the best spots is Gharghur at the eastern end of the Victoria Lines, a peaceful, elevated village with fine views of the coast and of the Lines. Many of the older houses in the village have been bought by young Maltese or foreigners and carefully restored. The elderly villagers who have sold their properties have been more than happy to move out to maisonettes with all mod cons on the edge of the village.

WIGNACOURT AQUEDUCT

When Alof de Wignacourt took on the role of Grand Master in 1601, his biggest headache was the desperate water shortage in Valletta. Water being plentiful around Mdina, he decided on the construction of an aqueduct stretching for 15km from the old city to the heart of Valletta. It was a huge and costly project which Wignacourt himself

Marigolds brighten the day in the Żebbuġ public gardens

partly financed. Stretches of this very impressive (but now disused) aqueduct can still be seen on the road from Valletta to Mdina.

ŻEBBUĠ

The name Żebbuġ means 'olives' and at one time the olive groves around here were prolific. Today Żebbuġ is approached by the De Rohan Arch, named after the penultimate Grand Master, Emmanuel de Rohan-Polduc (1775–97).

The town has several churches, the finest of which is St Philip, built in 1632 to accommodate the expanding parish and show off its wealth. It is thought to have been designed by Vittorio Cassar, son of Gerolamo, and there are similarities between this and the Co-Cathedral of St John.

Żebbuġ is also the venue of the world amateur billiards championship and, as the local guides will proudly point out, it is also the home of the former champion.

4.5km southeast of Rabat. Bus 88 from Valletta.

Mdina

The walk is a very short one, but at almost every step there is some fine mansion or architectural detail to admire. The route concentrates on the main street running through the town, but feel free to explore the narrow alleys off it. Mdina is so small you cannot get lost. *Allow 30 minutes.*

Start at the Mdina Gate, the main entrance to the city.

1 MDINA GATE

The triumphal gate was built in 1724 by Grand Master Vilhena to replace a drawbridge gate, the outline of which can still be seen to the right. The moat below you was first dug by the Arabs in the 9th century. Orange trees now thrive here and part of the ditch is given over to handball and tennis courts. On the far side of Mdina Gate look back to see the carved reliefs of the three patron saints of Malta: St Publius, St Paul and St Agatha. *Walk through the gate to the first square.*

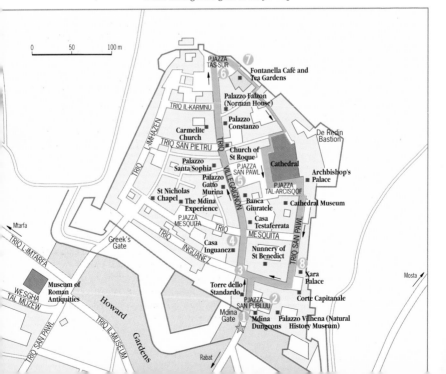

2 PJAZZA SAN PUBLIJU
(St Publius' Square)
The baroque Palazzo Vilhena (Vilhena Palace) on your right houses the Natural History Museum. On the left the stocky Torre dello Stendardo was once lit with fires to warn of landings by enemy troops. Today it is the police station.
Turn left, then right into the main street.

3 TRIQ VILLEGAIGNON
(Villegaignon Street)
This main thoroughfare has many fine *palazzi*. Look out for architectural details, such as window mouldings, shrines, reliefs and door-knockers.
A short way up on the left stop at the house with the huge Renaissance door-knocker with swinging nudes.

4 CASA INGUANEZ
This historic house is the home of Malta's oldest aristocratic family – the current baron's ancestors joined the upper echelons in 1350.
Walk on to the cathedral square.

5 PJAZZA SAN PAWL
(St Paul's Square)
The monumental twin-belfried cathedral dominates the square. Legend has it that this was the site of the house where St Paul converted Publius, governor of the island, to Christianity in AD60. The only odd building out on this fine baroque square is the Gothic-revival house, with gargoyles, built under the British.
Continue along Villegaignon Street, passing the very old Palazzo Santa Sophia on the left, the little church of St Roque on the right and, further up, the Carmelite Church with its distinctive belfry. Opposite, Palazzo Constanzo is open as a café and restaurant. Beyond is the Palazzo Falzon, one of Mdina's finest buildings (see page 65).

Mdina's triumphal main gate

6 PJAZZA TAS-SUR
(Bastion Square)
Pause to admire the magnificent panorama over half the island. You can see Valletta in the distance and on exceptionally clear days you can even spot Mount Etna on the island of Sicily.
Follow the ramparts to the right until you reach a sign saying 'Tea Gardens'.

7 FONTANELLA CAFÉ
This charming café occupies the garden of an old *palazzo*, from where you can enjoy yet more glorious views.
Continue along the ramparts, then a right and left turn will bring you back to St Paul's Square and the cathedral. Walk down past the cathedral into Pjazza tal-Arċisqof (Archbishops' Square) and follow Triq San Pawl (St Paul's Street) to the small square at its end.

8 XARA PALACE
The home of the Xara family for centuries, this fine old mansion has now been converted into a hotel. Today it is the only one inside the city walls. Opposite, the building with the figures of Justice and Mercy over the doorway is the Corte Capitanale, the former Courts of Justice. The dungeons lie below.
A right and left turn will bring you back to your starting point.

Buskett Gardens and Beyond

Beginning and ending in the Buskett Gardens, this ramble takes in a variety of landmarks from prehistoric caves and cart ruts to the Inquisitor's Summer Palace. The 6km walk will take you over rocky terrain, alongside sweet-smelling citrus trees, over streams and along the tree-lined paths of the Buskett Gardens. *Allow 2 hours.*

Start at the Buskett Forest Restaurant (bus no 81 stops near by). Turn right at the Grape and Wine Research Station, recognisable by the variously named vines growing beside it. After about 100m bear left and continue on this rough but metalled road until you see a sign for 'Cart Ruts', taking you to the right. Just before the road deteriorates, take the track to the right, going southwards over rugged limestone.

1 CART RUTS

The tracks in the limestone stretch from here to the Dingli cliffs. There are many theories about their purpose and age (see page 69). One is that the tracks were made by sledges or

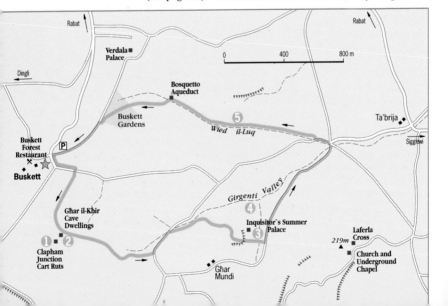

carts transporting stone from the nearby quarries.

Continue walking over the rugged terrain until you come to a large hole in the ground, on your left.

2 GĦAR IL-KBIR

The name means 'Great Cave', and if you scramble down the side of the pit you will find sizeable prehistoric dwellings which continued to be occupied until well into the 19th century.

Your next goal is the Inquisitor's Summer Palace, a squat grey building just visible on a distant hill to the east. More distinctive is the Laferla Cross to the left of it. Using the cross as your landmark, and with the caves behind you, follow the stone wall this side of the quarries. In places the path is non-existent, but if you make for the grove of carob trees, then bear left when a quarry blocks your path, following a fertile river bed, you should arrive – with a bit of scrambling – at a secondary road. For the palace turn left, then fork right under an arch.

Shady citrus groves in Buskett Gardens

3 INQUISITOR'S SUMMER PALACE

Guards will ensure that you get no further than the gates of the palace. It was built in 1625 and the caves below it were used as staff quarters – or so the story goes. For years it was abandoned and lay victim to vandals. Now it is being restored as a residence for the Prime Minister.

4 GIRGENTI VALLEY

The Inquisitors chose well, for the palace lies in the beautiful green Girgenti valley which is full of fragrant citrus groves.

To explore the valley, follow the track past the palace, then turn left at a little junction, passing citrus groves, then fertile fields. Beyond a newly constructed chapel, bear left and follow a small bamboo-filled valley

until you come to a little bridge over the Wied il-Luq.

5 WIED IL-LUQ

The river in this valley often dries to a trickle, or disappears altogether, but you can follow its course, where stands of bamboo grow up to 5m in height, back to Buskett Gardens.

A left turn immediately after the bridge will bring you up to the main road which you cross to join the right bank of the Wied il-Luq. Follow the riverbed until you come to the Bosquetto Aqueduct. Cross over the river for the path which leads back to the Buskett Gardens. If the aqueduct looks too narrow for your liking, you will have to scramble up the hillside, through farmland, then make your way back to the Buskett Gardens by road.

Southern Malta

Southern Malta stretches from Żabbar to Żurrieq. The region's coastline is characterised by numerous bays, inlets and creeks. It is an area of caves and grottoes, temples and towers, and of pretty bays as well as ugly ones – recent changes have made this a region of eyesores as well as beauty spots.

The seemingly endless conurbation stretching south and southeast of Valletta eventually gives way to agricultural land. Even here the villages are developing suburban tentacles that stretch further and further into the rural landscape.

For the visitor it is the coast that holds the attractions. Marsaxlokk, where traditional boats bob up and down on the intensely blue sea, is the prettiest of Malta's fishing villages. The fishing community still thrives here and the village manages to cope with the daily influx of summer visitors without yielding to the trappings of tourism. Southwest of the village the only decent sandy beach in Marsaxlokk Bay is spoilt by the proximity of the Malta Freeport.

Boat trippers are dwarfed by the huge scale of the Blue Grotto

In the south, where dried-up river valleys drop down to coastal cliffs, the star attraction is the Blue Grotto. From below the little village of Wied iż-Żurrieq, the local fishermen ferry visitors through this and other grottoes of the cave-riddled coastline.

To the southeast the region is rich in prehistoric sites. Għar Dalam, near Birżebbuġa, is a fascinating cave where the fossils of long extinct animals were discovered. Sadly, the famous ancient sites of the Tarxien Temples (see pages 102–3) and the Ħal Saflieni Hypogeum (see pages 98–9) are engulfed by suburbia; in contrast the ancient relics of Ħaġar Qim and Mnajdra in the south sit silently and mysteriously above the sea.

THE BLUE GROTTO

Given good weather, calm seas and an honest boatman (many charge more than they should), a boat trip along the dramatic cliffs of the south coast is one of the highlights of a visit to Malta. To see the grottoes at their best, try and make the trip on a bright morning, preferably before 11am when the sun is still low enough for the rays to penetrate the caves.

The boats ferry passengers from Wied iż-Żurrieq, a little fishing village on the south coast, reached by a spectacular drive along the cliffs. The traditional

With Nature as the architect, the Blue Grotto is a cathedral in stone

fishing boats run every day, provided that the waters are calm. In stormy weather the raging sea breaks on the headlands sending spray up to 30m or more into the air. This alone makes driving to the southern coast worth the trip.

The village of Wied iż-Żurrieq consists of no more than a cluster of houses and cafés, an exhibition of seashells, a small shrine giving heavenly protection to fishermen and a watch-tower erected by the Knights to warn of enemy ships sighted on the horizon. A slipway lined with fishing boats leads down to the miniscule harbour. This is a popular spot for swimmers and scuba-divers. Fishermen cram in as many visitors as

they can (eight is supposedly the limit), then set off for the 25-minute trip along the coast. The boats skirt weird-shaped cliffs and weave in and out of a series of caverns, each one with a different name. On a fine day the waters are constantly changing colours.

To reach the Blue Grotto itself (so-called because of the deep blue of the water inside) boats pass under a monumental arch, resembling a flying buttress. From here you glide into the dark grotto, which cuts 45m deep into the cliffside.

2km southwest of Żurrieq. For information tel: 826947. The official charge for a trip is posted up in the village.

The pretty cove of Għar Lapsi is a great place for a picnic and a swim

FILFLA

Lying 5km off the south coast of Malta, this tiny, rocky islet once served as a target for the guns of the British Navy and Royal Air Force. This target practice

Though Malta is a rocky and arid island, the soil still supports colourful blooms

devastated the island's birdlife, but since the islet was declared a bird sanctuary, the storm petrels, gulls and shearwaters have returned to breed. It is also home to a rare species of lizard, which manages to live among the rubble and the unexploded shells.

No public access.

GĦAR HASAN (Hasan's Cave)

There are many legends about this cave on the southern coast; all featuring the Saracen, Hasan, who took refuge here, and most of them referring to at least one young maiden that he abducted and imprisoned. The cave itself is no more than a long hollow in the limestone cliff. The woman who sits at the mouth of the cave will lend you a torch if you give her a tip. Otherwise take your own.

2km southwest of Kalafrana, well signposted from the Kalafrana/Żurrieq road.

GĦAR LAPSI

Not quite as pretty as it used to be, this is still one of the few spots on the south coast where you don't have to scramble down the cliffsides for a swim. It is also a good place for a picnic, with tables and benches laid out above the sea. The construction of a water treatment plant near by has not added to the attractions of the area though it is doing a useful job in helping to solve Malta's water shortage.

4km south of Siġġiewi. Bus 94 from Siġġiewi.

Malta's national bird, the blue rock thrush, has a beautiful song

FLORA AND FAUNA

Although Malta is essentially barren, it begins to come to life with the autumn rains. The dust is washed away and by Christmas the terraced fields are green with crops, and the citrus groves are laden with fruit. The early spring, lasting until April, sees a succession of wild flowers and herbs. Sprouting from the stony soil or seemingly solid rock are several varieties of narcissus, iris, gladiolus and marigold. Red and yellow poppies grow wild and the blossom of rock-roses dots the hillsides. In towns, pink and white-flowered oleander trees line the avenues, while bougainvillaea adds a dash of red or purple to the white walls of the villas and holiday homes.

All year round you will stumble across the very rampant Malta knapweed with its pale yellow flowers. Equally familiar is the fruit-bearing prickly pear cactus, seen growing wild by drystone walls or planted in hedges to provide sturdy protection for the crops.

Very few wild animals inhabit the islands. Wild rabbits live on St Paul's Islands and the occasional reptile may be seen, such as the chameleon or the rare Algerian whip snake. More common are the Moorish and Turkish geckos, which were introduced to Malta over 100 years ago and now live inside houses, helping to keep the insects at bay.

Malta's bird population has been drastically reduced by hunters and trappers (see page 161). The national bird is the blue rock thrush, prized for its mellow song – and therefore frequently trapped or robbed of its eggs. Seabirds, including yellow-legged gulls, storm petrels and shearwaters breed on the sea cliffs around the islands.

The best time for birdwatchers is spring and autumn when migratory birds stop off on their journey between mainland Europe and North Africa.

HAĠAR QIM AND MNAJDRA TEMPLES

These twin temple complexes occupy a spectacular site above the sea, looking out to the island of Filfla. The sites belong to the Tarxien phases of around 3000–2500BC, and there are similarities with the Tarxien Temples (see pages 102–3).

Haġar Qim

Haġar Qim means 'Standing Stones' and though the globigerina limestone has been badly eroded, especially on the seaward side, the site still retains megaliths of huge proportions. The largest is 7m by 3m, which – with a block from the Gġantija Temples on Gozo – is

Stones carved with swirling motifs and pitted decoration at Haġar Qim

the largest used in any of the temples.

When the site was excavated in the early 19th century, seven fat statuettes were found here, among them the so-called *Venus of Malta*, a headless clay figurine of a standing female nude of exceptionally generous proportions. This is now in the National Museum of Archaeology (see page 38), along with squatting stylised figures – also headless and extremely obese – and a four-sided limestone altar found in the temples.

The site is complex and irregular, made up of various chambers and passageways and with no obvious plan. Even so it is a pleasure just to walk around and spot some of the details, such as the mushroom-shaped tables flanking one passageway, the shrine in the outer wall, the oval opening that suggests an oracle chamber, the blocks

of stone covered with pitted decoration and the well designed temple façade.

An otherwise spectacular setting is spoilt by the fence around the site, but there are plans to improve the landscaping and turn the whole area into an archaeological park.

1.5km west of Qrendi, signposted off the main road. Standard opening hours (see page 185). Admission charge.

Mnajdra Temples

The setting of the Mnajdra Temples, closer to the sea and unfenced, is even more splendid and evocative than that of Ħaġar Qim. The three temples are protected by an outer wall of coralline limestone which is harder than the globigerina variety and therefore better preserved than the stone of Ħaġar Qim. Similar features to Ħaġar Qim are the stone altars, the corbelling (here even more pronounced) and the square holes suggesting an oracular chamber. The whole façade of the Lower Temple is covered with pitted decoration.

500m west of Ħaġar Qim – take the (unsignposted) footpath to the left of the entrance of Ħaġar Qim, going towards the sea. Permanently open. Free.

MARSASKALA

Set at the head of a narrow sheltered inlet, Marsaskala is steadily developing into a popular residential and tourist area. High-prowed, brightly painted *luzzus* (traditional boats) still dot the bay, but fishing is no longer its *raison d'être*. These days most restaurant owners in the village go to Marsaxlokk for the pick of the morning's catch.

On the headland south of the bay the Jerma Palace Hotel spreads out over the rocky shore, in front of the now incongruous-looking 17th-century St

Part of the complex of chambers making up Ħaġar Qim temple site

Thomas Tower. From here you can walk along the coast to Marsaxlokk.

To the annoyance of many locals a recyling plant has been set up on the main approach road to Marsaskala – next to a water treatment plant. This is part of a crucial project to cope with Malta's all-too-evident garbage problem.

South of Marsaskala, St Thomas Bay provides the only sandy beach in the area. This is too small to cope with the crowds and is currently spoilt by the holiday shacks along the front. Sheltered by white cliffs on the south side, the north side is given over to modern development.

Marsaskala is 11km southeast of Valletta. Bus 19 from Valletta.

The daily chore of unravelling the nets at Marsaxlokk, Malta's largest fishing village

MARSAXLOKK BAY

Though Marsaxlokk itself still retains its fishing-village charm, the character of its landlocked bay has radically changed with the advent of the Malta Freeport. The inappropriately named Pretty Bay at Birżebbuġa now looks out to berthing facilities that cater annually for around 200,000 container ships.

Always a vulnerable inlet, Marsaxlokk Bay has seen the arrival of a number of enemy fleets over the centuries. It was here that Turkish galleys first arrived in 1565 at the start of the Great Siege. It was here also that Napoleon and his troops landed in 1798, ending the Knights' rule on the island. More recently Marsaxlokk Harbour was the venue for the Bush-Gorbachev summit of December 1989 which symbolised the end of the Cold War. (The summit was going to take place in Valletta, but for security reasons, it was transferred to a warship moored in Marsaxlokk Bay and the sea was so rough that it was dubbed the 'Seasick Summit'!)

The charm of Marsaxlokk draws dozens of daytrippers, on coach or boat excursions. Happily though, the dearth of tourist accommodation has kept this very much a village rather than a resort.

BIRŻEBBUĠA

The town of Birżebbuġa, with its two bays, developed as a summer resort for the Maltese long before the present tidal wave of tourism. Originally a fishing village, it now sprawls all the way from St George's Bay, with its tiny beach, to Pretty Bay and Kalafrana beyond. The sandy beach at Pretty Bay is comparatively large for Malta and still draws the crowds despite the proximity of the Malta Freeport.

The bars and restaurants of Birżebbuġa still thrive and there are one or two hotels and guest houses. For most visitors the main draw is the fascinating

Ġhar Dalam cave (see page 92).
*10km south of Valletta. Buses 11, 12, 13
and 115 from Valletta.*

BORĠ IN-NADUR

The fortified settlement of Borġ in-Nadur
dates from the Bronze Age (around
1500–700BC) and once consisted of a
group of oval huts fortified by large
ramparts. Only vestiges remain but
shallow bottle-shaped pits, probably used
for the storage of grain or water, were
found close to the site on the edge of the
seashore, some of them actually
submerged. There are also cart tracks
(see page 69) which lead directly into
the sea.

There is no official entrance to the site
and the remains are inconspicuous. South
of the main road junction at St George's
Bay, take the right turn between the bus
stop and the public toilets. The first
turning right will bring you to the
remains.

DELIMARA

The long peninsula enclosing
Marsaxlokk Bay on its eastern side runs
down to Delimara Point where a
lighthouse stands. This is popular walking
territory, though less so since the
construction of a huge power station on
the Marsaxlokk Bay side. Its red and
white topped tower is a very conspicuous
landmark. The bay spreads out below
you, its waters intensely blue and inviting
despite spreading industry. The seaward
side of the peninsula remains unspoilt
and at Peter's Pool, signposted from the
road, you can sunbathe on smooth rock
shelves or dive down into deep clear
waters.

North of Peter's Pool, Ħofra Iz-Zgħira
and Ħofra I-Kbria are glorious horseshoe-
shaped bays where the cliffs drop down to

Students compare notes as they sketch
the attractions of Marsaxlokk Bay

crystal-clear aquamarine-coloured
waters. North of Ħofra I-Kbria, a radio
relay station dominates the headland and
a danger sign warns anyone with a
pacemaker to keep their distance.
Another sign forbids hunting but you
can't walk far before you stumble on a
spent cartridge or a caged bird left on a
drystone wall to lure others of its kind.

Squid for sale – a young entrepreneur offers
his wares in Marsaxlokk

Ancient stalagmites and stalactites deep inside Għar Dalam, the 'Cave of Darkness'

GĦAR DALAM

Għar Dalam, or the 'Cave of Darkness', gives its name to the first phase of Maltese prehistory (5000–4500BC). The cave was one of the earliest sites used by neolithic man who crossed to the Maltese islands from Sicily around 5000BC. Even more remarkable than the evidence of prehistoric man was the discovery of thousands of fossilised animal bones. The cave was discovered in 1865 by an Italo-German palaeontologist. Excavations revealed that the floor of the cave had five different layers. In the lower layers were enormous quantities of fossilised bones, tusks and teeth belonging to extinct species – such as dwarf elephants and dwarf hippopotami – along with red deer, brown bears, wolves, foxes and giant swans. In the upper layers archaeologists found flint tools, slingstones and pottery which had been decorated with the rippled edge of seashells or by pointed sticks or bones.

Long before archaeologists took any interest in this site, the remains of other prehistoric animals had been discovered elsewhere on the islands. In the distant past local Maltese believed they were the bones of the giants who were supposed to have built the island's megalithic temples.

The Għar Dalam cave is a wide, low tunnel which cuts 140m into the coralline limestone. Visitors can walk 80m into the cave, aided by electric lighting, and there are useful explanations of what was discovered where. On the cave bed you can still see layers of bone deposits.

At the entrance of the site a small museum displays a fascinating collection of teeth, tusks and bones from the thousands of animals found here. Interesting reconstructions show the size of extinct species such as the dwarf elephant.

The cave is signposted on the main Valletta/Birżebbuġa road, about 0.5km from St George's Bay. For information tel: 824419. Standard opening hours (see page 185). Admission charge. Buses 11 and 115 from Valletta.

KALAFRANA

Now dominated by container-terminal activities, Kalafrana used to be an important Royal Air Force base. Near by is the disused Hal Far airfield, used in World War II, where a couple of wrecked aircraft can still be seen.

Malta Freeport

The strategic location of Malta, and the

fact that it enjoys tax-free status, led to the establishment of the Malta Freeport in 1988. Marsaxlokk harbour, being the biggest on the island, was the obvious choice of venue. It is estimated that the number of containers being handled here will rise to 400,000 during 1993. Terminal 1 is being extended by over half its present size to provide more berthing space together with increased dry and oil-storage facilities. Activities carried out within the tax-free zone include storage, packing, labelling, breakbulk, freezing and assembling. The oil terminal came into operation in March 1992.

The busy harbour scene at Malta Freeport in Marsaxlokk Bay

THE EYE OF OSIRIS

The most eyecatching feature of a Maltese fishing village is the *luzzu*, a small high-prowed fishing boat painted in dazzling hues of red, blue, green and yellow. The boat may well have the name of a Catholic saint, but it will also be adorned, on either side of the prow, with the carved and painted eyes of a pagan god.

The custom of carving the ever-watchful eye, to ward off the devil and give protection to the little fishing boats, goes back centuries. The eye is that of Osiris, one of the most important gods of ancient Egypt. Legend has it that Osiris was drowned by the god Seth, who tore the corpse into 14 pieces and flung them over the earth. The goddess Isis found and buried the pieces, giving new life to Osiris. From then on he remained in the underworld as ruler of the dead and as the power that grants all life, springing through the soil from the underworld. Egyptian dynastic rulers believed that they became one with Osiris at death and thus became immortal.

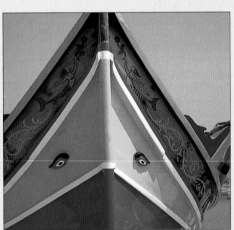

Superstition is a strong characteristic of the Maltese. Many of the churches have two clocks on their belfries, one telling the correct time, the other falsely set to confuse the devil and distract him from his evil intent. Many farms and country houses have bulls' horns tied on the roof to ward off the devil, often alongside or close to a holy image. After all, most Maltese are, despite their devout Catholicism, the inheritors of pagan ideas that long predate Christianity.

To spot Malta's traditional fishing boats, look in the busy harbours of St Julian's Bay, Marsaxlokk and in the Blue Grotto. Off-season you can see *luzzu* owners in the boatyards, touching up the scratches, adding a lick of paint or carefully defining that precious Eye of Osiris.

Fishing boats on Malta add their colour to many a waterside scene, and all are protected by the carved and painted eyes of Osiris, the ancient Egyptian god of the underworld and of immortality

Bobbing boats, painted in dazzling primary colours, catch the eye in Marsaxlokk

MARSAXLOKK

Lying at the head of the deepest inlet of the bay, Marsaxlokk is the largest fishing village on the island. The name comes from the Arabic *marsa* meaning 'harbour' and *xlokk* – the local name for the hot dry sirocco wind which blows from the Sahara. You still sometimes hear the village called (or see it written as) Marsascirocco.

The first sight to catch your eye as you explore the village will be the fishing boats that bob in the blue waters of the bay, painted in dazzling hues. On the quayside fishermen spread their nets, repair their fishtraps or touch up their boats for another day's work.

Adding to the colourful scene is the daily market, where lace and linen flutter in the breeze and stalls are hung with chunky knitted jumpers. The main market day is Sunday, when the harbourside is packed with stalls selling everything from cacti and caged canaries to pirated tapes and T-shirts. In season both Maltese and visitors arrive *en masse*, not just to buy at the market (the produce, apart from the fresh fish, is unremarkable) but to lunch out at one of Marsaxlokk's scores of restaurants. Naturally the emphasis is on fish, and each restaurant is likely to offer a choice of a dozen different dishes, ranging from squid to swordfish. To eat here at a weekend, it is wise to reserve a table in advance.

9km south of Valletta. Bus 27 from Valletta.

Tas Silġ

In the 1960s, when Italian archaeologists excavated the Tas-Silġ sanctuary, dedicated to the Phoenician goddess Astarte, they discovered not just Phoenician artefacts but also, in the layers beneath, evidence of Bronze-Age man. No one knows whether Malta was merely a convenient port of call for the Phoenicians or whether they established a fully fledged settlement on the islands; in either case the site provided the first evidence of probable co-existence between the prehistoric peoples already established on the islands and the Phoenician immigrants.

The ruins lie 1.5km east of Marsaxlokk, off the road going to Delimara Point, but are not open to the public.

MQABBA

Stone-quarrying is the main activity at Mqabba. Around here and Qrendi you can stop at the roadside and watch the limestone being cut before being carted off to building sites. Thanks to the softness of the newly quarried globigerina limestone, the blocks can be hewn using circular saws, eliminating any necessity for blasting. The great square holes, whose regular yellow walls look like sliced slabs of cheese, are an extraordinary sight. When the quarries are exhausted the holes are filled with earth and, in some parts of Malta and Gozo, used as vegetable plots. With one quarry closed another has to open, for it is limestone that feeds the never-ending building boom in Malta. Whether for a drystone wall or a seven-storey hotel, there are piles of pale yellow stone, blocking the pavements or stacked by the wayside, wherever you go in Malta.

10.5km southwest of Valletta. Bus 35 from Valletta.

QRENDI

This ancient village of narrow twisting streets has no less than four churches and one tower. The village is within walking distance of the Blue Grotto and the temples of Ħaġar Qim and Mnajdra. Built by the Knights, the Gwarena Tower on Tower Road is unique in being the only octagonal tower on the islands.

To the southeast of the village there is an extraordinarily large hole called Il-Maqluba which was created by the collapse of a series of caves. From a viewpoint you can look down on to the dense jungle of bamboo, bushes, carob and fruit trees that now fill the hole. As one of the few really fertile spots on the island, this is a mini-paradise for wildlife – and for the local children who scramble down the steps to collect the pomegranates.

11km southwest of Valletta. Bus 35 from Valletta.

Festive banners in the ancient and church-filled village of Qrendi

PAOLA

The suburb of Paola was officially established by Grand Master Antoine de Paule in 1626 to cope with the overspill from Valletta and the Three Cities. Today it is a sprawling residential and commercial town, which, with the notable exception of the Hypogeum and the temple ruins at neighbouring Tarxien, has little to delay the visitor. The original parish church of St Ubaldesca is not in use but there are many more recent churches including Christ the King, a huge mock-Romanesque structure built in the 1920s. The square in front is the scene of a busy morning market, held daily from Tuesday to Saturday.

ḤAL SAFLIENI HYPOGEUM

In 1902, when builders were digging a well on a site for new houses in Paola, they struck the roof of the upper floor of a huge complex of underground chambers. Rather than reporting their discovery to the authorities, the builders used the cavity for the disposal of rubble. It was nearly three years before the existence of this vast and remarkable labyrinth of chambers became common knowledge.

The excavations that subsequently took place were led by the eminent Maltese archaeologist, Sir Themistocles Zammit. On the lower level, the remains of 6,000 to 7,000 human bodies were discovered, along with personal ornaments and pottery. The precise purpose of the Hypogeum remains a mystery, partially because of the primitive methods then available to the archaeologists; it is generally thought that the temple complex was used as a burial site and as a sanctuary. Archaeologists

The interior of the Ḥal Saflieni Hypogeum

meanwhile dream of the discovery of another similar structure so that modern methods might throw light on the function of its individual features.

A tour of the Hypogeum is not really complete without a visit to the Archaeological Museum in Valletta (see page 38), which has a model of the site, and a collection of the statuettes and pottery that were found here. Covering nearly 800sq m, the chambers are built on three levels and descend to a depth of 12m. Tools made of flint, bone and hard rock were used to hack away at the limestone and create the chambers.

The highest level is the oldest, dating to around 3000BC. From here a modern spiral stairway leads down into the dimly lit and somewhat spooky centre of the complex (claustrophobics should steer clear). Here the carved walls, corbelled ceilings, large three-stone doorways and fragments of spiral decoration all re-create the architectural features of the temples above ground. Because the ceilings here are intact, it gives you a good idea of how the above-ground temples (all now roofless) must have once looked.

The chamber known as the 'Holy of Holies' reveals traces of red ochre on the walls, red being the colour of blood, sacrifice and death, suggesting that this was both a burial place and a shrine. The Oracle Chamber, where a square niche is cut into the wall, has remarkable acoustics. Deep (usually male) voices reverberate and carry to the far end of the chamber, while high female voices seem to have no effect at all. This is believed to be the cavity where the priest-oracle interpreted dreams. It was in these mid-level chambers that the so-called 'Sleeping Priestess' was discovered – a small statuette of a female with tiny head

The 'Sleeping Princess' may be a fertility figure

and fat body lying on a couch. This and other obese female figures, which can be seen in the Archaeological Museum in Valletta, suggests some sort of fertility cult.

Other items found in the Hypogeum include pots with abstract decoration and personal ornaments – such as a necklace (which has been reconstructed) made of pierced shells and beads.

From the middle level, an ancient and uneven staircase leads down to the lowest set of chambers. It was here, among the pits and tombs, that the remains of thousands of bodies were unearthed, along with their grave goods. *Triq Hal-Saflieni (Burials Street), Paola. From Valletta take the second main turning left, signposted to Paola, along Triq il-Palma. After about 1km turn right at the crossroads (with the Portelli Pharmacy on the corner). The first right turn (marked Hypogeum) will bring you to the entrance. The Hypogeum is currently closed for restoration. Tel: 825579 for the latest information. Once it reopens, access will be limited to 15 visitors at a time, so be prepared for queues. Admission charge (unlike all other state-run museums, this also applies on Sunday). Buses 5, 6 and 18 from Valletta.*

THE COPPERLESS

Malta and Gozo are justly famous for their temples and tombs. On the two islands, 34 prehistoric sites have been discovered, 23 of them being temples. Some of these, to the untrained eye, look no more than a pile of rubble or the remnants of a drystone wall. On the other hand, the finest examples demonstrate a remarkable sophistication and rank among the oldest free-standing structures in the world.

The first traces of civilisation on Malta date to around 5000BC when farmers sailed across from Sicily. These first inhabitants lived in caves, but around 4000BC a completely new way of life emerged. This was the era of the temple builders – known, somewhat misleadingly, as the Copper Age. The tools used at this time were made of flint and obsidian – no copper was ever discovered.

The exact function of the temples remains a mystery, but the most likely theory is that they were built as places of worship as part of a fertility cult. The most eloquent evidence of this is the excavated statues and figurines of

COPPER AGE

The ancient temples and cart tracks of Malta continue to mystify and enthrall visitors

remarkably obese females, thought to represent a goddess of fertility. Some of these sculptures are so abstract as to look remarkably modern – as do some of the decorated pots that have been discovered.

No two temples are the same, but all of them feature a series of horseshoe-shaped apses linked by a common passageway. A striking feature is the use of great monoliths, carefully crafted from limestone. These weigh several tonnes and were probably transported by primitive sledges, carts or pulleys and rollers (in this respect, the construction of the temples may be linked to Malta's famous prehistoric cart tracks – see page 69).

Malta's temple-building civilization came to a sudden end around 2000BC. Nobody knows quite why; perhaps because of hostile invaders, the plague or famine. What is very apparent is that the race which followed was barbaric by comparison; and the disappearance of the temple-builders marked the end of the greatest phase of Maltese prehistory.

Tarxien Temples

*O*nly a few hundred metres from the Hypogeum, the above-ground Tarxien Temples provide a striking contrast to those dark subterranean chambers, though the urban environs hardly make an appropriate setting for such age-old relics. This complex is the largest and most recent of the 'Copper Age' temples on Malta. It is also the most elaborately embellished. As in the Hypogeum no metal tools were used and the ornamentation, in the form of spiral reliefs and carved animals, suggests a sophisticated community of temple builders and carvers.

The complex was also the richest repository of prehistoric art on the islands, untouched for thousands of years until Sir Themistocles Zammit started his excavations in 1915. To see

The inner shrine, with its raised threshold carved with spirals

the statuettes and ceramics discovered here, and for an overall appreciation of the complex, it is essential to visit the Museum of Archaeology in Valletta (see page 38). The site comprises three main temples, with a fourth in ruins. The age of the temples is a matter of some controversy, though it is generally

believed that they were built between 3500 and 2500BC.

The temple complex is entered through the threshold of the South Temple, which was restored this century. Near the façade the large stone balls were used as rollers to transport the massive megaliths from which the temples were built. Inside the temple on the right is a statue of the lower half of a female figure, with a frilled skirt and obese legs. This is a copy of the original which is preserved in the Museum of Archaeology. The statue, which must have originally stood nearly 3m high and dominated the whole temple, is thought to have represented a fertility goddess. In the niches of this temple the bones and skulls of sacrificial animals were discovered and, still visible are the stones carved with a procession of what could either be sheep or goats. In the inner shrine a raised threshold, carved with an elaborate system of spirals, stands before the innermost part of the temple. Many of the decorations in the temple have been eroded by the elements and the decorated blocks you see here are mainly replicas of those now in the Archaeological Museum.

The Middle Temple was a later addition, built between the South and East Temples. Thick layers of ash were discovered here when the temples were excavated, along with cinerary urns and burial offerings. Experts believe that these were from the funeral pyres of late Bronze-Age invaders, a cruder, fiercer race of people who made use of the temples after the original neolithic builders had disappeared into oblivion. In a small room between the South and Middle Temples there are animal figures carved in relief on the walls. The two bulls and the sow suckling 13 piglets

More maze-like spirals decorate stone blocks throughout the temple complex

represent virility and fertility, the latter being a theme which constantly recurs within the temples. In the inner apses of the Middle Temple are more examples of spiral and pitted decorations.

The Eastern Temple has what is believed to have been an oracle chamber. The secret hole in the wall was probably used by a priest or priestess. The acoustics here are exceptional, as can be demonstrated if you call out in a low voice through the niche. The noise will reverberate through the temple and beyond.

Triq it-Tempj Neolitici (Neolithic Temples Street). The temples are not easy to find. From the Valletta direction take the second main turning left signposted to Paola; follow this main street as far as the monument, where you turn left. From here the temples are signposted. Tel: 433826. Standard opening hours (see page 184). Admission charge. In summer go early to avoid the crowds and the midday sun (there is virtually no shade). Buses 8, 11 and 26 from Valletta.

ŻABBAR

This old agricultural town, typically Maltese in character, began to prosper in the 17th century with the building of its huge parish church.

Our Lady of Grace

The sanctuary was begun by the prolific architect, Tommaso Dingli, though few of its original features survive today. The dome was badly damaged by French fire from the Cotonera Lines in 1800, aimed at Maltese insurgents who based themselves in Żabbar prior to attacking Valletta and the Three Cities. That dome was replaced with a fine new one which soars dramatically above the town. Suffering again in World War II, the church has since been restored to its former glory. A small museum contains *ex voto* paintings offered by those who have escaped disasters at sea, including Maltese slaves who managed to escape from a Turkish galleon and, more recently, those who were miraculously saved when a bus plunged over the rocks. Żabbar's church attracts many pilgrims and, on the eve of the *festa* of Our Lady of Grace, cyclists, motorcyclists and motorists (in that order) make the journey from Rabat.
Tel: 824383. Open: 6am–noon, 5–7pm. Museum open: Sunday 9.30–11.30am, but will open on other days if requested.

Żabbar Gate

The town is connected to the Three Cities by the triumphal Żabbar Gate, the finest of the gateways along the Cotonera Lines. The gate bears a bust of Grand Master Nicolas Cotoner (who funded the building of the Cotonera Lines), surrounded by a flurry of carved angels and war *memorabilia*.
On the Żabbar to Cospicua road.

Hompesch Arch

Not nearly as distinguished as the Żabbar Gate, this arch, which acts as a roundabout, was the last monument to be built by the Knights. It is named after the last of the Order's Grand Masters, Ferdinand von Hompesch.
Southwest of Żabbar, on the road to Paola.

ŻEJTUN

Żejtun means 'oil press' but nowadays there is not an olive tree in sight. What this ancient village has retained is two notable parish churches. The sombre and majestic Church of St Catherine, whose bold dome rises high above the town and its flat rural surroundings, is one of Lorenzo Gafà's finest achievements. It was built in 1692 and has been steadily embellished over the years. At one time it even earned itself the name 'Cathedral of the East'. The Church of St Gregory, in St Gregory's Road, is noticeably older and more mellow. It was built in 1436, then extended by the Knights – hence the miscellany of styles.
8.5km south of Valletta. Bus 27 from Valletta.

ŻURRIEQ

This large sprawling village and market centre is normally overlooked by visitors in a hurry to get to the Blue Grotto. It is one of the oldest villages in Malta and several of its buildings date from the days of the Knights. The Church of St Catherine boasts some of the finest paintings by Mattia Preti who lived here in 1675; sadly, like so many church paintings in Malta, these are too dark to appreciate fully.

On the edge of the village the small Armeria Palace, with a watch-tower at the rear, was built by the Knights and

The monumental Żabbar Gate carries a bronze bust of Grand Master Cotoner

used as an armoury. In the abandoned settlement of Ħal Millieri the late medieval Church of the Annunciation, with some notable murals, has been restored by the Malta Conservation Society.

Żurrieq is famous for its two summer *festas*. The festivities last several days with long processions through the streets and huge sums of money spent on spectacular displays of fireworks, which are made in a local factory.

10.5km southwest of Valletta. Buses 32 and 33 from Valletta.

Żabbar is 8km southeast of Valletta. Bus 19 from Valletta.

GOZO
Victoria (Rabat) • Mġarr
Mellieħa
Għajn Tuffieħa •
Mdina • Sliema
Rabat • Valletta
• Buskett
MALTA

Southern Malta

Variety is the keynote here – the tour takes in temples, fishing villages and coastal grottoes. The round trip is 64km. See map on pages 6–7 for route. *Allow a full day.*

From Sliema, follow the coast road south; after Msida Creek, at a major junction, follow the signs for Birkirkara (marked B'kara), then turn left at the Hospital sign. Follow the airport signs until you come to Paola.

1 PAOLA

Here you can see Malta's most famous prehistoric site: the Hypogeum (see pages 98–9).

From Paola head east to Żabbar, via the Hompesch Arch (see page 104) and follow the signs to Marsaskala.

2 MARSASKALA

Marsaskala (see page 89) has no sandy beach but you can swim from the rocks or sit in a café and watch the fishing boats. On

A pensive fisherman in the picturesque village of Marsaxlokk

the headland, opposite the Jerma Palace Hotel, stands the forbidding St Thomas Tower. It was built by the Knights in 1614, following a Turkish incursion here in the same year. Today it serves as a bar.

Take the main road south from Marsaskala (marked St Thomas Bay); turn first right, then left (marked to Marsaxlokk), then follow the signs to Delimara Point.

3 DELIMARA PENINSULA

Despite the power station (built in front of Dom Mintoff's seaside retreat) and the activities of the Malta Freeport, Delimara Peninsula still makes a spectacular vantage point. Peter's Pool, marked from the road, is an idyllic spot to swim off the rocks.

Retrace your route from Delimara Point and turn left at the small green-domed chapel for Marsaxlokk.

4 MARSAXLOKK

Stop for lunch at Malta's most picturesque fishing village – either a bite on the harbour front or fresh fish cooked Maltese style at Ir-Rizzu.

Continue round the bay, past St Lucian Tower and down into St George's Bay. A diversion to the right here will take you to the Għar Dalam Cave (see page 92). Continuing around the bay, stop at the monument on the seafront opposite the Pinto Battery.

5 GORBACHEV/BUSH MONUMENT

Opposite the Pinto Battery a monument commemorates the meeting in Malta of Presidents Gorbachev and Bush on 23 December 1989 – signalling the end of the Cold War.

Follow the coast road round to Pretty Bay. At the entrance to Malta Freeport bear right, past the Telemalta transmission stations.

Sunlight and water create colourful effects inside the Blue Grotto

Skirt the disused Ħal Far Airfield. Turn left at the junction and bear right along a secondary road to bring you into Żurrieq. At the main road turn left, following signs for the Blue Grotto and Wied iż-Żurrieq.

6 BLUE GROTTO

Before Wied iż-Żurrieq a roadside 'balcony' affords magnificent views over the sea and cliffs. Boats for the Blue Grotto (see pages 84–5) depart from the harbour of Wied iż-Żurrieq.

Leaving Wied iż-Żurrieq, rejoin the main road, turning left through barren hilly countryside and divert left for the spectacularly sited Ħaġar Qim and Mnajdra temples (see pages 88–9). After 3km turn left at a roundabout for Għar Lapsi.

7 GĦAR LAPSI

End the day at this cove beneath the cliffs. There is a tiny beach, a few fishing boats and a restaurant serving (among other things) the Maltese national dish of stewed rabbit (*fenek*).

Return to the roundabout and make the home journey via the church-dominated villages of Siġġiewi and Żebbuġ. From Żebbuġ, follow the signs for Valletta, then for Marsa and Sliema.

Northern Malta

*N*orthern Malta has a varied and heavily indented coastline. Until the British came the whole area was more or less uninhabited. Coastal attacks had forced the islanders to form their communities inland and the only structures of any significance were the coastal watchtowers built by the Knights.

St Paul's is one of the region's few settlements and in recent years it has grown from being a humble fishing village into a great hub of tourism. It was once a weekend retreat for the Maltese, who cut boat-houses out of the rocks and built small holiday homes by the sea. Now the development stretches, almost uninterrupted, for over 5km along the bay. The most heavily developed area is Buġibba, which, with its big apartment blocks and general air of tourism, resembles one of the Spanish costas.

Other stretches of the north are still unspoilt. Between Baħar iċ-Ċagħaq and Salina Bay, the only structures along the craggy coastline are a couple of towers. In winter, the only sign of activity is the fishermen who cast their lines from the rocks or wade waist high into the water. In summer, cars park along the coast road and the rocks are dotted with swimmers or people picnicking by the sea. Inland the scenery is noticeably barren, the only conspicuous plants being the agaves bowing to the wind.

Another quiet and seemingly remote region is Marfa Ridge, whose tip forms the northernmost part of Malta. The only developments here are the small resorts on the Comino side, where low-rise Maltese holiday homes dot small sandy bays.

The west coast has the loveliest and least-spoilt scenery: golden sandy bays separated by rugged headlands, cliffs providing fine walks and fertile valleys where you can still see horsedrawn carts and women hoeing in the fields. Drystone walls flank neat, sloping fields of vegetables and vines, while the country paths are strewn with wild fennel and caper bushes.

GĦAJN TUFFIEĦA

Għajn Tuffieħa is the name of the rugged stretch of coast west of Mġarr where three golden bays and a backdrop of spectacular cliffs combine to make this Malta's most desirable coastline. There is very little development and the hinterland is noticeably green in comparison to the rest of the island.

The rugged coastline at Għajn Tuffieħa is still undeveloped (but not undiscovered)

The Golden Sands Hotel overlooks Malta's finest and most popular beach in Golden Bay

Għajn Tuffieħa Bay is 3.5km northwest of Mġarr. Buses 47 and 52 from Valletta.

Golden Bay (Ramla Tal-Mixquqa)
Golden sands, aquamarine waters and ease of access make this the most popular of the three beaches. In summer months expect to step over myriad bronzing bodies to find a spare patch of sand. A good many of them will be staying at the Golden Sands Hotel, which lies north of the bay.

This is a good family beach, where you can windsurf, water-ski, tour in an inflated sea-sausage, ride by horse to the Popeye Village, or take a speedboat or cruiser to Comino's Blue Lagoon. The shallow, clear waters are tempting but take heed if the warning flags are up.

Għajn Tuffieħa Bay
This is the largest and the most beautiful of the three bays. The steps down the cliffside and the limited facilities deter many beachgoers and it is never as crowded as Golden Bay. A watch-tower stands on the promontory to the north and a derelict hotel overlooks the beach. Southwards there are fine walks along the cliffs (see pages 116–17).

Ġnejna Bay
Approached from the Mġarr road, the smallest of the three bays is easily reached by car. It is another pretty bay although the sands here are more shingly and the boathouses don't enhance the setting. If the beach is crowded make for the rocks to the north, which are sufficiently smooth for sunbathing.

From the bay the road to Mġarr passes through the pretty Ġnejna Valley, a fertile area where figs, bamboo and vines flourish.

MELLIEĦA AND ENVIRONS

Perched high on a spur, the village of Mellieħa overlooks the sweeping expanse of its bay and beach. It is a busy little shopping centre with more character and intimacy than the sprawling resorts to its east. The main steep street, lined with grocery shops, small bars and restaurants, caters for local residents as well as holidaymakers. Mellieħa has a wide range of self-catering accommodation, including luxury villas (one area of seaview villas is known as Millionaire's Valley). At the other extreme is a vamped-up cave dwelling cut into the rock above the road which zigzags down to the beach. One of several caves inhabited by troglodytes in the past, it was used as a bomb shelter in World War II and, according to some of the locals, is currently inhabited by the village eccentric.

Mellieħa has long been a favourite spot for the Maltese and more recently it has become popular, particularly with the British. Somewhat cut off from the island's main activity centres, the village and the little resorts of Marfa Ridge are well suited to those seeking relative peace, good walks, excellent swimming and boat trips to Gozo and Comino.

13km northwest of Rabat. Buses 43, 44 and 45.

Church of our Lady of Victories

The large parish church of Mellieħa stands sentinel over the bay, perched on a spur. Below it the fascinating Grotto of the Madonna is an intimate little marble chapel with an ancient fresco of the Virgin Mary. The locals claim it was painted by St Luke. In a side corridor there are numerous votive offerings to Our Lady in thanksgiving for cures and miracles.

Mellieħa Square. Open: weekdays 8.30am–noon, 4–6pm. Free.

Għadira Nature Reserve

In an effort to preserve both local and migratory birds from Malta's merciless hunters, the wetland inland from Mellieħa Bay (which is the only one of any real significance on the island) has been turned into a bird sanctuary. Resident species to look out for are black-winged stilts, avocets and Cetti's warblers. Among the migratory birds seen here are plovers, little stints, ruffs, redshanks, greenshanks and various types of sandpiper.

Open: daily 9am–4pm. Groups of 12 are taken in at hourly intervals.

Marfa Ridge

If you see Malta as a fish, Marfa Ridge is the tail. Here the sea views, the small sandy beaches and – for Malta – the surprising amount of greenery, combine to make excellent walking territory (see pages 118–19). From Ċirkewwa ferries ply across to Gozo, passing the little island of Comino on the way. The boats may be a little old-fashioned (they were imported second-hand from northern Europe) but they are perfectly adequate for this short and scenic trip. You can either sit on deck or inside the cafeteria where coffee, almond cakes and newspapers are sold. If the sea is really rough (and occasionally in winter waves splash right across the slipway at Ċirkewwa), boats depart from St Paul's. Ċirkewwa is also the departure point for boats to Comino. These are more like fishing boats than ferries – and the boatmen often trail a line through the waters as the boat crosses the channel.

South of Ċirkewwa, Paradise Bay has an attractive, but small and crowded, sandy bay.

Ċirkewwa is 5.5km northwest of Mellieħa. Bus 45 from Valletta.

Mellieħa Bay

Also known as Għadira Bay, this is the biggest sandy beach on Malta. Extensive sands and good beach facilities draw the crowds from spring to autumn. It is one of the best beaches for children as it slopes very gently. Water-sports enthusiasts are well catered for with paragliding, windsurfing, water-skiing, sailing and canoeing.

The drawbacks are the busy main road running behind the beach and the unsightly green complex of chalets on the far side of the bay. Erected without planning permission, these holiday homes may prove not to be a permanent feature of the seascape.

1.5km northwest of Mellieħa village.

Popeye Village

The Popeye Village at Anchor Bay is where the 1980 film of *Popeye* was shot. The ramshackle village by the sea consists of 17 houses, all made of wood imported from Canada and the Netherlands. It took a force of 165 men, eight tonnes of nails and 9,000 litres of paint to create the set. The latest addition is a film shown on the site about the making of the film. Amenities include a souvenir shop, snack bar and beach facilities.

2.5km west of Mellieħa at Anchor Bay. Tel: 572430. Open: summer 9am–6pm, off-season 9am–5pm. Admission charge.

The Popeye Village film set

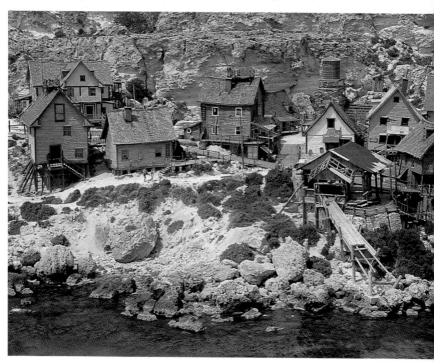

The eerie wind-eroded remains of the Skorba Temple ruins

MĠARR

The dominant feature of this village is its huge church (see page 117). The other main reason for visiting Mġarr is to see the nearby prehistoric temples.
6km northwest of Mosta. Buses 46 and 47.

Skorba Temples

Tall megalithic blocks and scanty ruins mark the site of one of Malta's very earliest settlements. Excavations here in the 1960s revealed that neolithic man had built a small village of huts, made of wattle-and-daub on low stone foundations. This is the only such settlement on Malta which has been fully investigated. There are also the fragmentary ruins of two later temples which were probably once roofed over.

Various types of pottery were found on the site and these gave their names to the Red Skorba phase (4400–4100BC) and the Grey Skorba phase (4500–4400BC). Pots, vases and fragments of figurines unearthed here can be seen in the National Museum of Archaeology in Valletta (see page 38).
1.5km east of Mġarr, on the outskirts of Żebbieħ. Although the site is not officially open to the public, the key is available from the National Museum of Archaeology in Valletta (see page 38).

Ta'Haġrat Temples

These two prehistoric temples are similar to those of Skorba, though not quite as old. The remains are scanty and only of real interest to experts and enthusiasts.
In Mġarr, signposted off the road to Mosta. Closed to the public but visible from the gate or key available from the National Museum of Archaeology in Valletta (see page 38).

ST PAUL'S BAY (San Pawl il Baħar)

Several sites around this bay recall stories of St Paul's sojourn in Malta, among them Għajn Rasul (Apostle's Fountain) on the coastal road which is said to be the spot where St Paul struck a rock which promptly spouted water; and the parish Church of St Paul (Our Lady of Sorrows) which is supposed to be the site of the spot where St Paul shook off a viper into the fire.

St Paul's itself sprawls inelegantly along the main coastal road. Though it is not as blatantly tourist-orientated as Buġibba (see page 114), it has lost its former fishing-village charm and its older buildings look somewhat forlorn. The prettiest spot is the harbour, though even here the view of fishing boats is gradually giving way to one of construction.

Fishing boats now bob in the bay where St Paul was shipwrecked

Near by, the Wignacourt Tower is one of the few reminders of the days of the Knights. A more modern landmark on the seafront is the Gillieru restaurant, where catamarans draw up for some of the best fish and seaviews in the region. The restaurant has seven of its own boats for fishing.

17km northwest of Valletta. Buses 43, 44, 45 and 49 from Valletta.

ST PAUL'S SHIPWRECK

According to the Acts of Apostles (Chapter 27), St Paul and St Luke were on their way to Rome to be tried as political rebels when their ship foundered on the rocks of Malta. The actual site of the shipwreck is generally thought to have been one of the islets to the north of St Paul's Bay. The Apostles were welcomed by the islanders and for an entire winter they sheltered in a cave at Rabat. From here St Paul preached the Gospel, converting the Roman governor, Publius, who became the first Bishop of Malta.

The islet of Selmunett is today distinguished by a huge statue of St Paul. The island is uninhabited but you can hire a boat or swim across for a closer look – it is only about 200m from St Paul's Bay. Once a year the Maltese sail over in fishing boats to celebrate open-air mass by the statue.

Watery adventures at the Splash and Fun Park

Buġibba

The architecture does not inspire, but Buġibba is probably the cheapest place to stay on the island. Although somewhat cut off from Valletta and from other main parts of the island, its facilities are such that many of its visitors are happy to stay put. The emphasis is on bars, pubs, discos and restaurants (mainly of the pasta, pizza and hamburger variety). A lively promenade offers bathing and a variety of watersports, including paragliding. On summer evenings the streets teem with people and music blares from late-night bars.

Daytime activities include boat trips to the islands of Comino and Gozo. Another popular tour is the Underwater Safari; portholes below sea-level allow you to view the world of marine fauna and flora as you steam round St Paul's Bay. There are also views from the boat of the statue of Christ, commemorating the visit of Pope John Paul II who paid a visit to Malta in 1990.

Underwater Safari departures: five times a day from Buġibba's il-Menqa, next to Bognor Beach. Pick-ups are available from Sliema and St Julian's. Reservations can be made through hotels or any travel agent or through Captain Morgan Cruises, Dolphin Court, Tignè Seafront, Sliema. Tel: 331961. Bus 49 from Valletta to Buġibba. Buses 48 and 51 connect Buġibba with St Paul's Bay.

Mistra Bay

This sheltered inlet on the northern side of St Paul's Bay affords good swimming from the rocks. Mistra Village, overlooking St Paul's Bay and the relatively green Mistra Valley, is one of the island's more desirable self-catering complexes. The Mistra Sports Club, within the village, offers tennis, squash and swimming.

Qawra

Together Qawra and Buġibba now occupy almost the entire peninsula on the east side of St Paul's Bay. More or less merging with Buġibba, Qawra is more restrained than its noisy neighbour, with a choice of slightly more superior accommodation. Hotels and apartments have been mushrooming here since the 1970s and continue to do so. Among the hotels here is the New Dolmen, named after the megalith which stands, somewhat incongruously, in its gardens.

Like Buġibba, there are plenty of bars, cafés and restaurants. The rocky beach has a restaurant and plenty of facilities for watersports enthusiasts. The Qawra Tower at the far end of the peninsula was one of many fortress towers erected by Grand Master Martin de Redin in the 17th century.
Bus 49 from Valletta. Buses 48 and 51 connect Qawra with St Paul's Bay.

Salina Bay

East of St Paul's Bay, Salina Bay cuts deeply into the coastline. At the head of the bay are disused salt pans. They look like shallow trays cut into the stone and were first used by the Knights in the 17th century. The west side of the bay is dominated by the highrise development of Qawra, including the big and brash Suncrest Hotel, the largest resort hotel on Malta.

Value for money is an important part of Buġibba's appeal

SPLASH AND FUN PARK

You can't miss this huge complex, set on a quiet stretch of coastline. It is Malta's only leisure park and it provides activities for children of all ages: a large water chute, a playground with dinosaurs, a pool with dolphins, a swimming pool, funfair rides, train rides and bouncy castles.

Baħar iċ-Ċaghaq, 9km northwest of Valletta. Tel: 375021. Open: daily 10am–dusk, but winter openings depend on the weather. Admission charge. Bus 68 from Valletta.

Għajn Tuffieħa Seascapes

Għajn Tuffieħa is hard to beat for cliff scenery and dazzling blue seas. This walk follows the clifftops, then turns inland to the village of Mġarr where you can lunch on rabbit stew. From Mġarr you can complete the circuit either by walking along the road or taking a bus to Valletta. The full circuit on foot is 8km. *Allow 2 hours.*

Start at the Golden Sands Hotel at Ramla Tal-Mixquqa (Golden Bay – bus 47 or 52 from Valletta). Beyond the Apple's Eye Café, take the track to the right which brings you to the clifftop. Follow the path to the tower on the headland.

1 GĦAJN TUFFIEĦA

At the headland stop to savour the magnificent seascape of Għajn Tuffieħa. It was here in 1565, just prior to the Great Siege, that 181 Turkish ships lay at anchor, awaiting a change of wind before landing at Marsaxlokk. The beach of Għajn Tuffieħa is arguably the loveliest on Malta.

Follow the path round to the car park above the beach. Beyond the

Nearby

1 Ġnejna Beach

2 Skorba Temple

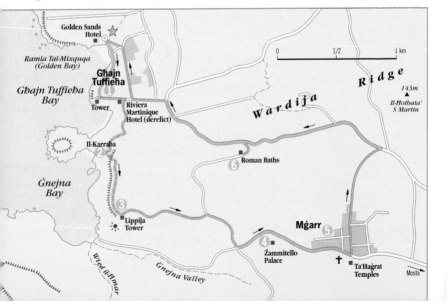

derelict Riviera Martinique hotel take the
path to the right over the cliffs. Keep to the
ridge all the way, avoiding the path lower
down the cliffs.

2 IL-KARRABA

The sea has chiselled weird and
wonderful geological features along this
coast. Il-Karraba (the Battleship) is the
name given to the prominent, strange-
shaped headland where boys fish with
home-made bamboo rods; the 'Dinosaur'
is the name of the ridge which gives
access to it. Beyond Il-Karraba, rocky
ledges provide a secluded spot where
topless sunbathers flout the law.

*Keeping to the ridge and scrambling over the
occasional outcrop, continue walking along
the coast.*

3 LIPPIJA TOWER

When Ġnejna Bay comes into view, head
for the tower, which stands slightly
inland. This was one of the several
watch-towers built to defend the coast
against Turkish attacks. In spring the
ground around here is strewn with wild
flowers.

*Just before the tower, pick up a rough track
leading inland, with views over the Ġnejna
Valley. The silver-topped dome of Mġarr's
church soon comes into view. Turn right
when you reach a narrow metalled road,
and follow it for 0.5km. At the minor
crossroads turn left for Mġarr.*

4 ZAMMITELLO PALACE

This elegant little mansion comes up on
your right as you approach Mġarr. It
belongs to the same family which owns
the smaller islet in St Paul's Bay.

5 MĠARR

The disproportionately large church was
funded from the sale of poultry and eggs

The magnificent landscape and clear blue
seas around Għajn Tuffieħa

– hence the ovoid shape of the dome.
Various cafés and bars cluster around the
church square. 'Friends to All' does a
good rabbit stew. A little way off the road
to Mosta, signed from the square, you
can visit the Ta'Hagrat Temples (see
page 112).

*From Mġarr you can take bus 46 or 47
back to Valletta. Alternatively you can
return to Golden Bay by foot using the
roads. Take the left turn beyond the church
and after 1km left again towards Għajn
Tuffieħa. Continue walking until you see
below you, on the left, a complex of ancient
ruins.*

6 ROMAN BATHS

These remains were unearthed in 1929
when a local was digging for water and
UNESCO spent large sums of money
restoring the site in 1961. A friendly
woman sits by the gate and will show you
round the relics of steam baths, water
channels, lavatories, changing rooms,
swimming pool and mosaics.

*After 1km turn left at the junction, then
right for Golden Bay; this is well-signposted
and the Golden Sands Hotel is a
conspicuous landmark.*

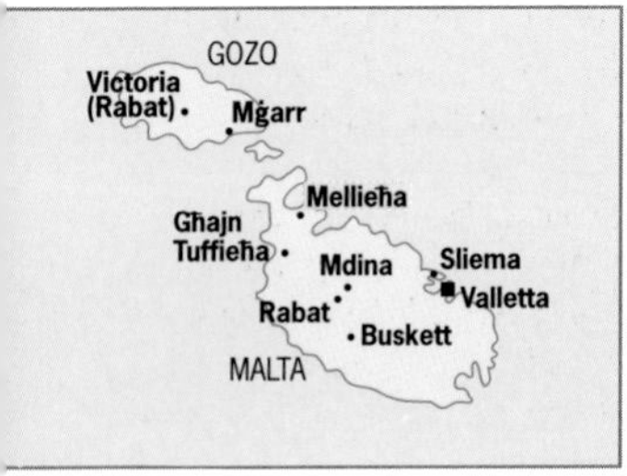
GOZO
Victoria (Rabat)
Mġarr
Mellieħa
Għajn Tuffieħa
Mdina
Sliema
Valletta
Rabat
Buskett
MALTA

Marfa Ridge

This exposed ridge of northern Malta provides fine seascapes, cool breezes and sufficient shade from trees and shrubs to shelter you from the midday sun. ***Allow 3 hours for this 9km walk.***

Start at the Armier crossroads, reached by the bus 45 to Ċirkewwa from Valletta. If you are coming from Mellieħa, look for the landmark tower southwest of the crossroads.

1 THE RED TOWER

On the crest of the Marfa Ridge, the gaunt weathered tower (now more pink than red) was built by the Knights in 1649 to guard against pirate raids and the possible return of the Turks. *From the crossroads take the pot-holed ridge road that runs in a northeasterly direction. Ignore any minor tracks to the left running down to the South Comino Channel and follow the road as far as it goes. After 2km you will come to a picnic area shaded by acacia and eucalyptus trees where you can enjoy the views over the bay. Continue to the end of the road.*

Nearby

1 Mellieħa village and beach

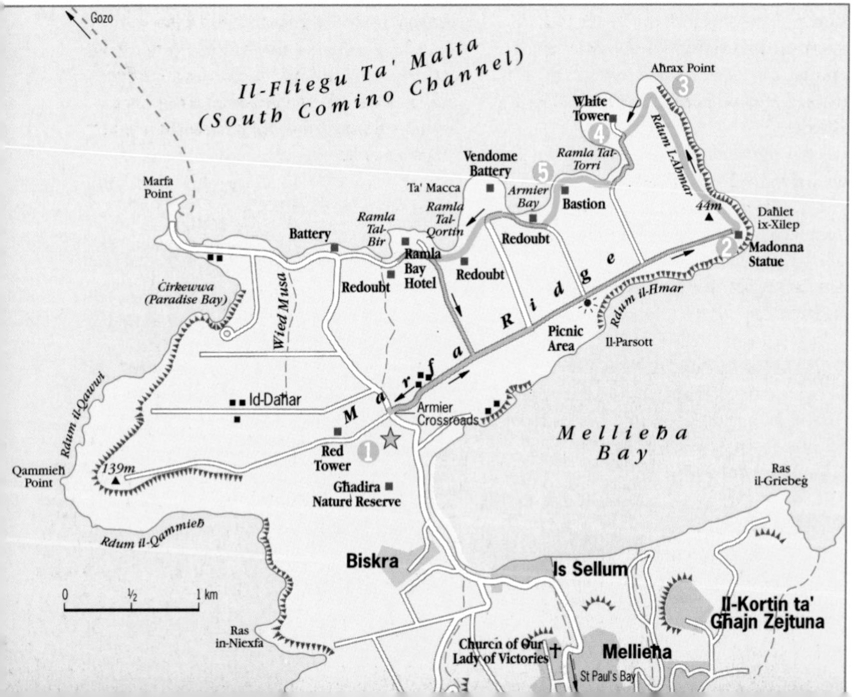
Gozo
Il-Fliegu Ta' Malta
(South Comino Channel)
Aħrax Point
White Tower
Rdum L-Aħmar
Ramla Tat-Torri
Vendome Battery
Ta' Macca
Armier Bay
Bastion
Ramla Tal-Qortin
Ramla Tal-Bir
Battery
Ramla Bay Hotel
Redoubt
Redoubt
Redoubt
44m
Daħlet ix-Xilep
Madonna Statue
Marfa Point
Ċirkewwa (Paradise Bay)
Wied Musa
Marfa Ridge
Rdum il-Ħmar
Picnic Area
Il-Parsott
Id-Daħar
Armier Crossroads
Mellieħa Bay
Red Tower
Għadira Nature Reserve
Rdum il-Qawwi
Qammieħ Point
139m
Rdum il-Qammieħ
Ras il-Griebeġ
Biskra
Is Sellum
Il-Kortin ta' Għajn Zejtuna
0 ½ 1 km
Ras in-Niexfa
Church of Our Lady of Victories
Mellieħa
St Paul's Bay

2 THE MADONNA STATUE

The end of the ridge road is marked by a lonely Madonna and a tiny chapel replacing an older one that is now in ruins. This windswept but spectacular spot above the sea is rarely deserted. On fine days ramblers picnic among the pines, and homing-pigeon enthusiasts release their flocks, while hunters and trappers go for anything that flies. Out to sea you can normally spot at least one huge tanker on the horizon or the ferry plying between Valletta and Gozo.

Turn left and walk along the headland, making your way over rough coralline limestone, scattered with tiny white snail shells. The cliffs gradually give way to less dramatic rocky shores where fishermen cast out their lines into the vividly blue waters.

3 AHRAX POINT

At this most northerly tip of Malta beware of the great oval cavernous hole, about 25m long and 14m wide, whose depths are filled with dark-looking waters.

From here walk south towards the White Tower.

4 THE WHITE TOWER

The tower and the redoubts punctuating the coast used to be the only structures

on Marfa ridge. Now the bays on this side of the ridge are dotted with an assortment of Maltese holiday homes and shacks.

Work your way along the coast, savouring the seaviews and stopping for a dip at one of the sandy bays. Beyond White Tower, Ramla Tat-Torri (Slug Bay) is far more inviting than it sounds.

5 ARMIER BAY

The two sandy crescents of this bay have become quite popular in summer and you·will find beach facilities, pedaloes for hire and simple cafés. In winter it is more or less deserted

At the end of Armier beach, beyond the car park, turn left; then, where the main road angles, go straight on, thereby cutting across the Ta'Macca headland. Skirt the small beach of Ramla-Tal Qortin, passing some boat-houses and head on to the Ramla Bay Hotel. This has its own little sandy beach, a seaside pool and watersports facilities available to non-residents. The views across to Comino and Gozo are particularly fine. Take the minor road from the hotel to the ridge road, then turn right to return to your starting point.

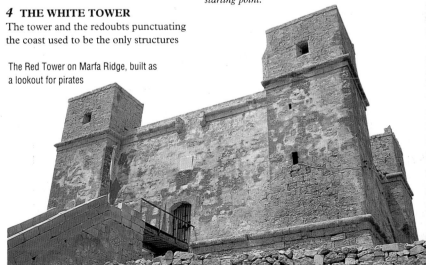

The Red Tower on Marfa Ridge, built as a lookout for pirates

Northern Malta

This 60km tour takes you along the varied coast of northern Malta, round bays, over ridges and down to the golden sands of the west coast. See map on pages 6–7 for route. *Allow a full day and be prepared for traffic jams, especially on summer Sundays.*

From Sliema follow the coast road to St Julian's, where Spinola Bay is studded with fishing boats. Going up the hill follow the signs for St Andrew's, and join the main road. Rejoin the coast again at Baħar iċ-Ċagħaq, where the waterchutes of Splash Park catch the eye. The road then follows an undeveloped stretch of rugged coastline.

1 SALINA BAY

Rounding Għallis Point, where a lonely tower stands guard over Salina Bay, the modern blocks on the far side hit the eye. Skirt the disused salt pans at the head of the inlet and just after the

bay, stop at the Kennedy Memorial Olive Grove. Here a simple, evocative monument, standing among trees and shrubs, commemorates the assassination of US President John F Kennedy in 1963. *Follow the signs to St Paul's Bay and reach the harbour by turning right after the Agip petrol station, opposite a fish shop. At the harbour turn left, keeping to the coast and stop at the coastal tower.*

2 WIGNACOURT TOWER

Grand Master Wignacourt was responsible for this and many other early 17th-century towers. It is currently being renovated to form a museum about St Paul. From here there are good views of St Paul's Islands, where the Apostle was shipwrecked. *Take the fourth street on the left to rejoin the main road. Turn right and follow the road down to Pwales Beach. Climb up through Xemxija, down into the Mistra Valley and zigzag up towards Mellieħa. Before the village, turn right at a roundabout marked Selmun Palace.*

3 SELMUN PALACE

This fortified villa was built in the 18th century as a country retreat. It is closed to the public but occasionally opens for banquets, weddings and art exhibitions. The 4-star Maritim Selmun Palace Hotel alongside echoes the palace in style. There are fine walks over the headland and, if you take the track opposite the chapel and scramble down the cliffside, you will find a delightful hidden beach.

4 BELLEVIEW BAKERY

Rejoining the main road to Mellieħa, stop on the edge of the village at the

Belleview Bakery for some of the best and crustiest bread in Malta. *In Mellieħa, stop to see the village and church (see pages 110–11), then zigzag down to its large beach. This same road will take you to Marfa Ridge. Turn right along the ridge road and drive until you can go no further. Stop by the Madonna for splendid seascapes then return to the roundabout on the far side of Mellieħa's beach and take the steep twisting wide road uphill marked Għajn Tuffieħa. At the next roundabout take the rough road to the right.*

5 GĦAJN TUFFIEĦA

Scenically this is the best part of the tour. A huge sweep of the west coast, with its cliffs and fertile hinterland, comes into view as you approach Għajn Tuffieħa. Crops, vegetables and vines flourish on the valley slopes, creating, along with the drystone walls, the effect of a colourful patchwork. *Choose Golden Bay or Għajn Tuffieħa for a swim or a walk along the sands, then take the inland road to Żebbieħ. From there, follow the signs for Mosta, whose dome looms above the village. Return to Sliema following the signs to Valletta, Msida and finally Sliema.*

Tiny fields surrounded by drystone walls characterise the north of Malta

Gozo

*L*ying just 6km off the coast of northern Malta, Gozo is often assumed to be a smaller version of its sister island. In some ways it is: the neat fields sheltered by stone walls, the flat-roofed houses and the dazzling blue waters surrounding the island are all reminiscent of Malta. At the same time it is noticeably more peaceful and rural, the pace of life is slower, the land is greener, the streets are cleaner and the coast is quieter. Looking over the wide valley and sweeping sands of Ir-Ramla (Ramla Bay), it is easy to see why the Gozitans (among other contenders) have always claimed theirs as the fabled Island of Calypso where the sea-nymph held the Greek hero, Odysseus, captive for seven years.

Gozo was, for centuries, the victim of marauding Arabic and Turkish pirates. Gozitans were often killed or taken off into slavery, leaving the population much depleted. Unlike Malta, Gozo has not made a living from trade. Farming (and to a lesser extent fishing) has always been the main activity of the islanders. That is why the villages were tightly packed on the hilltops to leave the slopes and valleys for intensive cultivation of vegetables and fruit. The irregular-shaped plots still necessitate simple methods of farming. The donkey carts, primitive ploughs and field workers wielding hoe and scythe are part of the charm of the landscape.

Flat-topped hills and baroque domes dominate the skyline. In villages the houses catch the eye for their elaboration – whether they are old buildings with finely carved balconies or new ones with twisted columns or ornate carvings. The houses of returned emigrants can be spotted by their carved kangaroos, maple leaves or effusive names such as 'God Bless America'. Gozo also has a fair number of old farmsteads, some expertly renovated by foreigners, one or two by film stars.

Getting around Gozo presents no

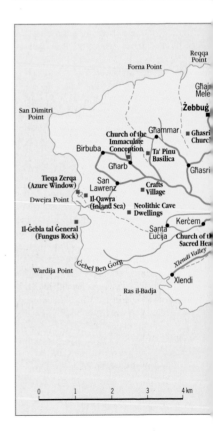

difficulty. All roads radiate from the capital, Victoria, and the signposting is good. Most visitors come for the day from Malta, taking in Victoria, whose handsome citadel sits on a hill at the island's centre, the finely preserved prehistoric temples of Ġgantija and the fishing villages of Xlendi or Marsalforn. Those who give the island more time or choose to stay here and explore its coastline and landscape will discover there is far more to the island than these well-known spots.

Gozo is tipped to be a fashionable haunt in the future. The completion of a 5-star hotel in Mġarr, the demolition of a tiny hotel in Xlendi to make room for a 100-bed 4-star establishment and plans for a large tourist village near Mġarr are all signs that this small, unspoilt island may, in years to come, lose its simple charm. If rural simplicity appeals, hurry to see the island before it's too late.

For ferry, hovermarine and helicopter services from Malta to Gozo, see **Practical Guide**_, page 187._

GOZO AND COMINO

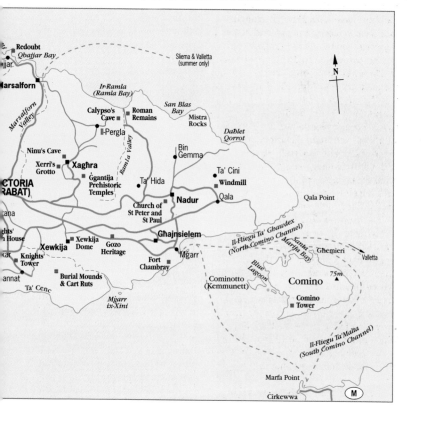

Victoria

*T*he capital and the hub of the island, Victoria combines an impressive hilltop citadel and a lively town below. The name was given to the city in 1897, on the occasion of Queen Victoria's jubilee; but to the Gozitans – and many Maltese – it will always be Rabat; that name means suburb and, as with Mdina and Rabat on Malta, the town here is a suburb of the fortress.

Victoria is a place to visit rather than to stay. One hotel and one guest house are the only accommodation and there are very few places to eat at night.

THE CITADEL (Il-Kastell)

Crowning a flat-topped hill, the great bastions of the Citadel dominate central Gozo, sheltering within its walls the cathedral and several museums. The Knights refortified the ramparts and used the Citadel as a refuge against attacks by Turks and pirates. At one time the entire

Victoria's hilltop citadel rises from sheer rocky cliffs

population of Gozo was able to shelter within its walls.

Parts of the Citadel are currently undergoing much-needed restoration. Until the task is complete (which will be many years hence), the sound of limestone blocks beings chiselled and sawn will be heard within the walls.

Archaeological Museum

The 17th-century Palazzo Bondi makes a fitting setting for Gozo's archaeological finds. Exhibits range from fragments of prehistoric pots to Roman *amphorae* and pottery found on shipwrecks off the coast of Gozo. The museum has a model of the Ġgantija temples (see page 134) and excavated finds from the site, including a stone phallus.
Triq Il-Ħabs (Prison Street). Tel: 556144. Standard Gozo opening hours (see page 185). Admission charge.

Cathedral

The fine classic façade of the cathedral, raised above a flight of steps, makes a powerful impact as you step inside the citadel. The cathedral was designed by Lorenzo Gafà, and built between 1697 and 1711 to replace an earlier church destroyed by the 1693 earthquake. It is one of the best examples of baroque vernacular architecture in Malta and was the Knights' own conventual church on

Gozo; on two occasions it served as the venue for the sumptuous investitures of the Grand Masters.

Compared to the relatively restrained exterior, the inside is very ornate. Tombstones decorate the nave floor and baroque paintings cover the walls of the side chapels – but the most fascinating aspect is the *trompe-l'oeil* painting which very convincingly (at least from the nave) creates the illusion of a large dome. The roof, as you can see from the ramparts, is in fact flat. Funds were insufficient for a real dome so, in 1732, the Italian artist, Antonio Manuele of Messina was commissioned to paint a false one.

The Statue of Santa Marija (left as you enter the church) was originally selected in Rome as a statue suitable for parading along the streets during local

> Victoria is reached by bus 25 from Mġarr harbour.

festas. When the Madonna arrived from Rome it is said that 'the people wept in satisfaction'. In 1956 the statue was formally donated to the cathedral and embellished with a diamond necklace, a solid gold belt and, six years later, a solid silver plinth donated by wealthy Gozitan emigrants. So highly regarded was the statue that a large modern arch was cut into the city wall in 1956 to make room for her entry into the Citadel.
Pjazza Katidral (Cathedral Square). Tel: 556087. Opening hours depend on visiting groups, but the usual times are 10am–4pm/5pm daily, but closed on Sunday afternoon. Free.

VICTORIA (RABAT)

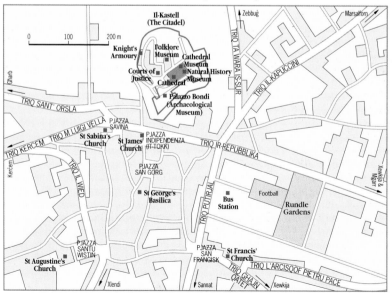

Market day in Gozo's main square, Pjazza Indipendenza, known as It-Tokk to locals

Cathedral Museum
At the back of the cathedral, this museum houses a modest collection of vestments, religious paintings, church ornamentation and old manuscripts; there is also a horse-drawn carriage which was used to transport the Bishop of Gozo on special occasions in the 19th century.
Triq il-Fosos (Fosse Street). Tel: 556144. Standard Gozo opening hours (see page 185). Admission charge.

Crafts Centre
This is a permanent and extensive display of Gozitan crafts. The items on view are not for sale but the cards of the artisans who made them are available.
Citadel. Tel: 556160. Free.

Folklore Museum
This is a charming museum where exhibits are laid out in the rooms of three late-medieval houses. The emphasis is on everyday Gozitan life over the centuries.

The exhibits cover crafts, costumes and farming implements.
Triq Bernardo De Opuo (off Triq il-Fosos). Tel: 562034. Standard Gozo opening hours (see page 185). Admission charge.

Knights' Armoury
The Knights made this their armoury in the late 18th century; it was then used as a British garrison in the 19th century and during World War II. Today it houses a small collection of historic weaponry.
Triq il-Kwartieri (Quarters Street). Standard Gozo opening hours (see page 185). Admission charge.

Natural History Museum
This small and informal museum is housed in a restored medieval building. The exhibition focuses on the geology and marine life of the island, and includes displays of fossils, fish and coral.
Triq il-Kwartieri (Quarters Street). Tel: 556153. Standard Gozo opening hours (see page 185). Admission charge.

IT-TOKK (Main Square)

It-Tokk means the 'meeting place' and for centuries this tree-lined square has been the hub of town life in Victoria. Every weekday morning stalls are laid out with fish and fruit, linen and knitwear, rolls of fabric and T-shirts. Around the square, shops sell chunky jumpers and bars serve potent Gozitan wine. Within the square is a bronze statue of Christ, erected to commemorate the Gozitan servicemen and civilians killed in World War II. Bordering the square is the 18th-century Church of St James (currently undergoing renovations) and the semi-circular Banca Giuratale, built in 1733 by Grand Master de Vilhena and now used as government offices.

Well worth exploring are the medieval alleyways behind the square in the old part of the town. The houses have some interesting architectural features and the tiny shops and bars here provide plenty of local colour.

ST GEORGE'S BASILICA

The solemn majestic Basilica of St George dominates its little square behind It-Tokk. Built in 1673, the church was badly damaged in the earthquake of 1693 and has been extended and embellished over the centuries. Sometimes called 'the Golden Basilica', its rich interior is profusely gilded and the centrepiece is a dominant bronze canopy, imitating that of Bernini's at St Peter's in Rome.

Pjazza San Ġorġ (St George's Square). Tel: 556377. Open: Monday to Saturday 5am–noon, 3–7pm. Free.

TRIQ IR-REPUBBLIKA
(Republic Street)

This was once known as Racecourse

Gozitans are adaptable people with an easygoing attitude to life

Street because horse trotting races used to take place here and still do on main *festa* days. The finest feature of the street is the series of handsome houses and overhanging enclosed balconies, some of them beautifully carved.

At one end, the Rundle Gardens provide a welcome respite on a hot day. On 15 August, the feast of the Assumption (called Santa Marija locally), this street is also the venue for an agricultural show, attended by large numbers of Gozitans, Maltese and visitors. If you want to see it, be there early – everything packs up by mid-morning.

WINE TASTING

At no 4 Triq il-Fosos (Fosse Street), close to the cathedral, stop to taste Ricardo Zammit's home-made red and white wines. These are served with Gozitan bread, cheese and tomatoes. Apart from bottles of wine you can also buy Gozitan honey, pottery, lace and other local crafts.

DWEJRA COAST

Cliffs, caves and freaks of nature combine to make Dwejra's seascape the most spectacular in Gozo. In calm weather the deep, clear and intensely blue waters are excellent for diving, snorkelling and swimming. Here, too, you can see the oldest salt pans on Gozo, from which salt is still collected in summer.

Azure Window (Tieqa Zerqa)

Thousands of years of erosion by the sea have created this monumental limestone archway at Dwejra Point. The long ledge of rock forming the upper arch of the

Wind, rain and waves have combined to create the Azure Window

'window' is in danger of collapsing – not that this deters geologists and others from walking across it to scan the rocky ledge for fossilised sea creatures.

Fungus Rock

The plant that once thrived on this steep-sided offshore rock was prized by the Knights for its medicinal properties – so much so that they jealously guarded the islet and made it inaccessible. The only way of reaching the virtually unscalable rock was by means of a hoist from the still-standing Qawra tower to the top of the rock. Any unauthorised person found attempting to gain access was sentenced to death.

The plant was pulverised by mortar and pestle, mixed with a little wine and

syrup and taken as a cure for dysentery and haemorrhages.

The local name for the island – Il-Ġebla tal-Ġeneral, the General's Rock – is said to commemorate an Italian general who, while supervising the quarrying of the rock in the Middle Ages, fell off the cliffside and drowned.

The Inland Sea (Il-Qawra)

Inland from the Azure Window, this pool of aquamarine seawater is surrounded by high limestone cliffs and linked to the sea by a narrow rock tunnel. It even has its own shingle beach and when the open sea is rough (which it frequently is) this provides a sheltered, shallow spot for bathing. In calm weather, fishing boats can be hired for a trip through the tunnel and along the cliffs near the Azure Window.

Dwejra Point is 5.5km west of Victoria. Bus 91.

GHARB

On the west side of the island, Għarb is one of Gozo's prettiest and most peaceful villages. Particularly fine features of the houses are the stone balconies, many of them old and finely carved. Several expatriates have made their homes here, restoring the old village and its farmhouses.

The dominant feature of the village centre is the baroque Church of the Immaculate Conception, whose concave façade, with its floral decoration and sculptures of Faith, Hope and Charity, makes a powerful impact. Two famous characters of Għarb are venerated in tiny museums: Frenċ tal-Għarb, Gozo's best-known faith healer, and Carmela Grima, who heard the miraculous voices at Ta'Pinu (see pages 132–3).

3km northwest of Victoria. Buses 2 and 91.

The Inland Sea remains tranquil even when the open sea is stormy

MARSALFORN

From a seaside village frequented by a small number of prosperous Gozitans, Marsalforn has now become Gozo's largest resort. The fishing village has gradually extended along the crescent-shaped rocky bay, and these days hotels, apartment blocks and souvenir shops are more prominent than the few fishing boats that dot the little harbour. The small shingle beach attracts the crowds but the bays of Qbajjar and Xwieni to the northwest are much quieter for swimming.

The salt pans all around here date from 1740 and are still in use, producing several tons of sea salt every year.

MĠARR

Arriving in Gozo from Malta, your first close-up view will be of Mġarr, where fishing boats and ferries are anchored in the harbour and flat-roofed houses climb up the hillside behind. Dominating the scene are the Gothic-style Church of Our Lady of Lourdes, perched on the craggy cliffs above the village, and the large church of neighbouring Għajnsielem. Modern development continues apace, the latest addition to the village being the 5-star hotel that sits conspicuously on the cliffs. To the southwest the walls and bastions of Fort Chambray (page 139) crown a promontory above the harbour.
6km east of Victoria. Bus 25.

The Gozo Heritage

In a converted Gozitan farmhouse, between Mġarr and Victoria, a series of reconstructed historical scenes takes you through 7,000 years of the island's chequered history. Events are portrayed by lifesize figures in period settings. A shop sells handmade Gozitan crafts.
20 Mġarr Road, Għajnsielem – well signposted on the main Mġarr/Victoria road. Tel: 551475. Open: daily 10am–5pm. Admission charge.

Calypso's Cave features in Homer's *Odyssey*

NADUR

The name of the town comes from the Arabic word meaning 'look-out point'. Clinging to a ridge 152m above sea level, Nadur was the chief watch-tower for the whole east coast during the time of the Knights.

The size and splendour of the 18th-century baroque parish church, dedicated to Saints Peter and Paul, gives you some idea of the prosperity of the place. Seafaring activities made it rich and gave the locals a certain superiority over the rest of Gozo (or so it is said). In the early 17th century Grand Master Wignacourt used the woods and gardens that then flourished here as his private shooting domain. Few dared to trespass; the penalty for poaching was to spend three years rowing in a galley.
6km east of Victoria. Buses 42 and 43.

QALA

This quiet rural village east of Nadur has one of Malta's few surviving (but no longer working) 19th-century windmills. To the east, where the coastline is characterised by cliffs and rocky outcrops, there are fine views across to the rocky island of Comino and the tiny isle of Cominotto beside it.
7km east of Victoria. Buses 42 and 43.

RAMLA BAY (Ir-Ramla)

North of Nadur, Ramla Bay has a splendid stretch of ochre sands, its green-blue waters protected by a rugged headland. Given the ease of access and the fact that it is the only sandy beach of any size on Gozo, it is not surpising that the bay draws Gozitans and foreigners in large numbers during the summer months. Beach facilities include cafés, watersports and sunshades. Even so, care must be taken if you intend to do more

Fishing for crabs and lobsters in Gozo's Mġarr harbour

than sunbathe: a notice on the beach warns swimmers of dangerous currents and reefs.

In the nearby Ramla Valley, the terraced fields, divided by bamboo fences, create a patchwork effect and lend an impressive backdrop to the bay.

Calypso's Cave

This is claimed by the Gozitans as the abode of Calypso, the sea nymph who enchanted Odysseus on his journey home from the Trojan War. The cave has since become blocked by boulders and now amounts to no more than a crevice on the cliff. In the *Odyssey* Homer describes Calypso's Cave as being surrounded by poplar and cypress trees, with a grape-laden vine at the opening. The best thing about the cave today is the breathtaking view over Ramla Valley and bay.

Ramla Bay is 6.5km northeast of Victoria. Bus 42.

SAN BLAS BAY

The steep narrow track down to this quiet little beach is almost inaccessible by car, but you can walk down and you will be well rewarded. There is no development here apart from a few boathouses and the bay is a perfect spot for a picnic or a dip. Dividing San Blas from the pretty little bay of Daħlet Qorrot are the awesome Mistra Rocks.

8km east of Victoria.

Formidable prickly pear hedge and
Ta'Pinu Church

SAN LAWRENZ

This is a clifftop farming village, on the
far west side of the island. From here a
spectacular road descends through arid
countryside to Dwejra Point. For many
years San Lawrenz was home of the
British author, Nicholas Monsarrat who
wrote the bestselling book, *The Kappilan
of Malta*. The author died in 1979 but
his wife still lives in the village and his
book sells in all the shops on the islands.

East of San Lawrenz you can buy
local handicrafts at the Ta'Dbieġi Crafts
Village and watch the artisans at work.
4km west of Victoria.

SANNAT

A quiet agricultural village in southern
Gozo, Sannat is one of the few places
where you can still see lace being made.
In the summer months you may see
elderly women seated outside their
doorways making shawls, tablemats or
lace-edged handkerchiefs. Sannat is also
known for its carved stone balconies.
These days the most conspicuous are the
brand new ones, with their ornate and
fanciful decoration. The focal point of
this straggling village is the twin-belfried
parish church, dedicated to St Margaret
and built in 1718 on the site of a smaller
church.

Beyond the village the sheer cliffs of
Ta'Cenc drop 180m down to the sea.
On the promontory lies the 5-star Hotel
Ta'Cenc – justifiably considered the
most desirable hotel on the Maltese
islands. Just one-storey high and built in
the local honey-coloured limestone, it
blends well with its surroundings. Not
far away the cart tracks and dolmens are
evidence of a prehistoric settlement.

From Sannat, a 1.5km walk along a
country road and then a valley will bring
you to the pretty little inlet of Mġarr ix-
Xini (see page 139).
2km south of Victoria. Bus 50.

TA'PINU

A centre of pilgrimage for Gozitans and
Maltese, the modern neo-Romanesque
sanctuary of Ta'Pinu rises majestically in
isolated countryside. The original church
was a simple 16th-century single-cell
chapel, looked after by a pious individual
called Fillipino Gauci – or Pinu for short.

In 1883 a local peasant woman called
Carmela Grima heard a mysterious voice
as she walked home to Gharb. She
entered the chapel to pray and again
heard the voice, commanding her to say

three *Ave Marias*. The only friend she told, Francesco Portelli, also claimed to have heard the voice several times. These incidents were followed by a series of miraculous cures in the neighbourhood and a year later Gozo escaped the plague that had struck Malta.

As a result numerous offerings were made to the chapel and with these funds, a new church was built integrating the old chapel. In 1932 Pope Pius IX raised Ta'Pinu to the status of a basilica. Since the end of the 19th century the church has been a place of thanksgiving for those saved from disasters or miraculously healed. In a side corridor there are paintings of shipwrecked sailors being saved and reminders of miraculous cures. At the altar you can pick up a 'petition',

listing the various favours you can request from Our Lady of Ta'Pinu (such as 'better position', 'raise in salary', 'sale of property', 'cure of alcoholism', 'Catholic boyfriend' and 'happy death'. The relevant box or boxes are ticked and the petition envelope, with money enclosed, is placed in a basket under the altar.

Opposite the church, climbing up the Għammar Hill, is a set of 14 life-size statues in marble, representing the Stations of the Cross.
4km northwest of Victoria, between Għammar and Għarb. Open: daily 6.45am–12.30pm, 1–6.30pm (Sunday to 7.30pm). Buses 61 and 91.

Marble statues representing the *Agony in the Garden* at Ta'Pinu

XAGĦRA

The huge and ornately embellished baroque Church of our Lady of Victories forms the focal point of this sprawling hilltop village. Every year on 8 September, the anniversary of the end of the Great Siege of Malta, the wraps come off the chandeliers, the silver and damask are displayed and a statue of the Virgin is paraded through the streets. Like all good *festas*, it ends with a dazzling display of fireworks.

Festivities aside, the main magnet of Xagħra is the site of the neolithic Gġantija Temples on the edge of the village.

Like many Gozitan villages, Xagħra is rapidly expanding and its new houses are made conspicuous by their elaborate architectural features. The village square is the social centre, with locals, expatriates and tourists congregating at the Oleander Restaurant for genuine Maltese home cooking.

For visitors looking for a base in the area, the 4-star Cornucopia Hotel, converted from a farmhouse on the edge of the village, is a particularly desirable place to stay.

3km east of Victoria. Buses 64 and 65.

Gġantija Temples

The setting of these prehistoric temples, affording a glorious panorama over a wide sweep of Gozo, is worth a visit in itself. 'Gġantija' means gigantic and there is a legend that the temple complex was built by a female giant who carried the stone blocks on her head from Ta'Cenc. When you see the size of the megaliths you will understand why it was assumed that no mere mortal could possibly have moved them. The outer walls of the temples are built with colossal horizontal and upright blocks, some of them reaching a height of 7.5m and weighing up to 50 tonnes. Size apart, this complex of two temples, surrounded by a common outer wall, is impressive for its state of preservation. The temples date from 3600–3000BC and rank among the finest in Malta.

The Gġantija Temples

The South Temple is the older of the two. On the left before you enter you will see the spherical stones which were used as rollers to transport the slabs. Just inside, on the left, is a recess, once filled with water, where worshippers washed their feet before entering the temple.

The temple interior consists of a smooth-walled limestone passage (once plastered and painted with red ochre) leading to the five apses; here you can see the remains of altars where rituals were celebrated and animals slaughtered. The blocks across the central apse formed the main altar and it was here that two stone heads, probably representing the goddess of fertility, were unearthed (they are now in the Museum of Archaeology in Victoria).

The apse to the left has two libation holes hewn out of the limestone at the rear of the chamber and on the right there is a curious hole at the foot of a monolith which may have been an oracle hole. Another apse contains the so-called 'Pubic Triangle' which was once partnered by the stone phallus that is also in Victoria's Museum of Archaeology.

The North Temple is smaller, with four apses. Built around 3000BC, it is not as old as the South Temple, but its state of preservation is not as impressive. *On the edge of the village, well signposted off the road from Victoria and reached by a short walk from the car park. Tel: 553194. Standard Gozo opening hours (see page 185). Admission charge.*

Ninu's Cave

The grandfather of the present owner came across this cave in 1888 while searching for water. The cave, below the owner's house, is small but has a forest of stalactites and stalagmites.

Xagħra Windmill is an elegant survivor of the many that once covered Gozo

Triq Jannar (January Street). Open: daily 8am–7pm. Admission charge.

Xagħra Windmill

Built in 1725, this is one of Gozo's few surviving windmills. The mill has been restored and the interior made into a museum, with an agricultural theme. *Triq il-Mithna (Windmill Street). Standard Gozo opening hours (see page 185). Admission charge.*

Xerri's Grotto

The father of the priest who owns Xerri's Grotto discovered this cave 70 years ago. It is larger and more varied than Ninu's Cave. The priest will point out shapes resembling a turtle, a turkey, a giraffe and a pair of elephant's ears. *Triq L-Għar ta'Xerri (Xerri's Grotto Street). Open: weekdays 9.30–11am, 2.30–4.30pm. Closed: Sunday. Admission charge.*

The mighty dome of Xewkija's church dwarfs everything around it

XEWKIJA

The mighty Xewkija rotunda, along with Victoria's citadel, is the most conspicuous landmark on Gozo. The dome is one of the biggest in the world – yet, for the Gozitans, it is not quite big enough; the intention was to exceed the dimensions of the Mosta dome in Malta, which it succeeds in height but not in diameter.

The church was built between 1951 and 1971, during which time services were held in the old baroque church. On completion the older structure was pulled down and all you can see of it today are some relics in the Church Museum.

The exterior of the church has been compared to the Salute in Venice; the proportions and the baroque style are certainly reminiscent, though the external decoration is not as abundant. *3km southeast of Victoria. Pjazza San Gwann Battista (Baptist's Square). Tel: 556793. Church open: 6am–noon, 3–8pm. Buses 42 and 43.*

XLENDI

The deep Xlendi valley runs down to one of the prettiest creeks on the island. The idyllic landlocked bay and the glorious blue-green waters have long been a haunt of artists and photographers. More recently it has become something of a tourist resort, the village expanding to take in self-catering apartments, villas, more than 10 restaurants and even a 4-star hotel. It is enormously popular and in summer gets very crowded, and even noisy. Nevertheless it still manages to exude local character and undeniable charm.

The shingle beach, rocky shore and clear waters are good for swimming and the caves and rugged reefs provide ideal conditions for snorkelling and scuba diving. On the cliff-side a series of steps, with beautiful bay views, lead to a small secluded pool which was once so private and little known that the local nuns used to come and bathe.

Xlendi looks its best in the early morning or at dusk when the daytrippers have gone. Ideally you should stay for an evening meal for Xlendi is liberally endowed with good eating places and the sunsets over the cliffs can be spectacular.

Some of the restaurants on the seafront specialise in local fish and succulent giant prawns.

Għajn il-Kbira

As you come into Xlendi from Victoria, you will pass by a public wash-house, (known as the Knights' Wash House) where the local women used to do their laundry. It used to be said that the spring waters here were the sweetest on Gozo.

Xlendi is 3km west of Victoria. Bus 87.

ŻEBBUĠ

Sprawling over a hilltop, Żebbuġ commands good views over the coast. From the village, a rough road zigzags down to the north coast and its shoreline is characterised by numerous salt pans. Examples of Gozitan onyx marble, which is still quarried here, can be seen in the village church.

3km north of Victoria. Buses 90 and 91.

The pretty harbour at Xlendi resembles a giant swimming pool

Gozo's Southern Shores

Step off the ferry at Mġarr and within minutes you can be striding out over the cliffs enjoying some of Gozo's loveliest coastal and valley scenery. The total distance is 7.3km. *Allow 3 hours.*

The walk starts behind the car park at the ferry terminal in Mġarr. Take the steps to the left of the bar by the tourist office and head westwards, along the coastal path.

1 TAFAL CLIFFS

The cliff path takes you past boulder-strewn shores, salt pans and secluded coves. On the landward side, small sloping plots are sheltered by drystone walls, bamboo fences or clumps of prickly pear. Keep to the coastal path all the way and ignore any tracks going inland. At one point the path is impeded by a stone wall and you will have to scramble uphill beside the wall, until you find a gate in the wall. From here you can rejoin the path.

Nearby

1 Xewkija Dome

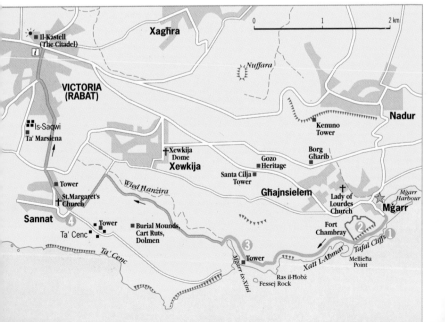

When the first set of salt pans comes into view, make towards the corner turret of Fort Chambray and pick up the path just below it.

2 FORT CHAMBRAY

Fort Chambray was the last stronghold to be built by the Knights. Planned in 1723 as a fortified town, complete with streets, church, town square and governor's palace, the work was never fully completed; it was only through the private funds of a French Knight, Jacques François de Chambray, that the fortifications finally materialised 26 years later. In more recent history the fort has served as a British garrison, a mental hospital and a tourist complex. The latest plans are for a 200-bed tourist village, which could change the nature of this quiet stretch of coast.

By the time you reach the western end of Fort Chambray, the beach and boathouses of Mellieħa Point will appear below. Keep to the path, which takes you down clay slopes past salt pans on the shore. Beyond here the track passes a high hedge of prickly pears, then follows a stone wall where cages containing small birds are perched during the trapping season.

3 MĠARR IX-XINI

The squat, semi-derelict tower which soon comes into view is your next landmark. It guards the entrance of the calm, fjord-like inlet of Mġarr ix-Xini, which is reputed to be one of the harbours used by the Knights' galleys. Today it is one of Gozo's prettiest coves – ideal for a dip, a picnic or a boat trip. To reach the cove, cross the clover-strewn slopes and dip down to the coast across more salt pans. All along there are splendid views of distant cliffs.

Follow the inlet as far as you can, along a

Fort Chambray, strategically sited on top of Tafal Cliffs

drystone wall. On the landward side of the 'beach', scramble alongside another smaller wall, sloping down the side of the valley. A flight of steps cut into the rock brings you down to the inlet. Next take the minor road on the far side of the inlet which climbs uphill, following the beautiful valley called Wied Ħanżira. The huge dome which soon comes into view is that of Xewkija church (see page 136). After 2.5km, bear left at the junction for the village of Sannat.

4 SANNAT

The agricultural village of Sannat is known for its lacemaking (see page 132). Before reaching the centre, savour the view to your right of the flat-topped hills, the church domes and the citadel of Victoria crowning a hilltop to the north. *In Sannat turn right for the church and the road that will take you to Victoria (2km). Alternatively you can take bus 50.*

Religion

*C*ombine the islands of Malta and Gozo and you have a church or chapel for every day of the year. This is perhaps not surprising given how devout the Maltese are. Since AD60, when St Paul was shipwrecked on Malta, religion has formed the solid base of Maltese life. Even for non-churchgoers (the young in particular are kicking their heels against the power of Catholicism), the Church is still the focal point of community life.

The vast majority of Maltese marry in church and attend mass at least once a week. Many will also pop into their parish church during the week. In some of the villages, churches open as early as 5.30 so that farmers can attend mass before the day's work begins. In Valletta the Church of St Paul's Shipwreck is open between 11am and 1pm for the benefit of workers in the city who want to attend mass during their lunch hour.

Religion is instilled in children from an early age. They are taken to church from the cradle. First Communion is a major event, and Maltese girls attend religious instruction before marriage. Once married, always married – in Malta divorce is against the law.

The parish church, be it baroque, classical or neo-Gothic, is invariably the largest edifice of any village, often totally out of proportion to the needs of the community it serves. Locals dig deep into their pockets to finance the building of newer, bigger churches, in some cases replacing a perfectly sound and adequate historic church. Big means best and village rivalry comes into play as one parish tries to outdo the next in size and embellishment of its church. The Maltese and the Gozitans will, for example, still argue over which has the biggest dome: Mosta or Xewkija.

Corpus Christi, an important feast in the Catholic calendar

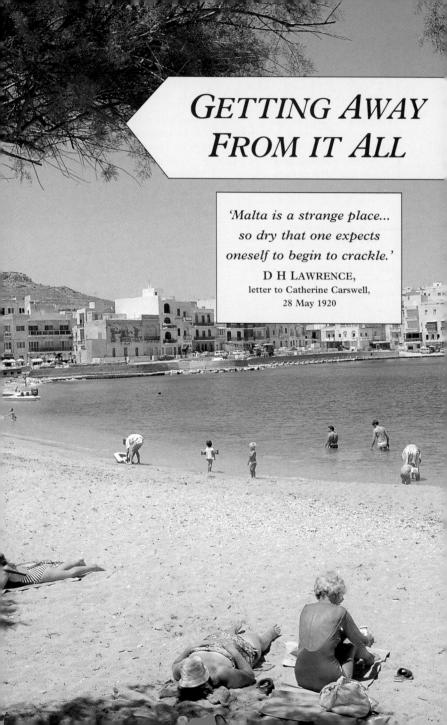

GETTING AWAY FROM IT ALL

'Malta is a strange place...
so dry that one expects
oneself to begin to crackle.'

D H LAWRENCE,
letter to Catherine Carswell,
28 May 1920

Getting Away From it All

Malta is so small that there are very few places, if any, which can truly be called 'undiscovered'. In the summer months even so-called 'secluded coves' will see a good smattering of locals and tourists, whether they be sunbathing on the beach or in a boat near by or scuba-diving among the rocks. Peace and tranquillity will only descend once the daytrippers have gone home.

One way to find peace and solitude is to take to the countryside or the cliffs by foot. This is not the ideal way of getting around in the heat of the summer, but out of season it's the best way of discovering the beauty spots of Malta. More rural than Malta, Gozo offers far greater opportunity for finding peace and quiet. The ferryloads of visitors who descend daily on its shores normally concentrate on the island's highlights, leaving the isolated spots for the more independent-minded visitor.

Comino is the quietest island of the Maltese archipelago (see page 144). Officially it only has three residents, so you can well and truly get away from it all!

BEACHES

Most sandy beaches are packed in summer. However, on Gozo, access to the pretty San Blas Bay is sufficiently tricky to deter the majority. At Mġarr ix-Xini, on the south side of Gozo, you can swim in the transparent waters of a deep inlet (see page 139). On Malta your only hope of finding a quiet spot is by scrambling down cliffsides or walking sufficiently far from main bathing areas.

PARKS AND GARDENS

Malta has an abundance of playgrounds but a scarcity of parks and gardens. The most popular place for picnics, or walks in the shade of the trees is the Buskett Gardens near Rabat (see page 69). The only other public gardens of any size are those of the San Anton Palace in Attard (see page 74). These are worth visiting for their avenues of trees and flowers, but access entails a drive through the Valletta suburbs.

JEEP SAFARI – GOZO

For exploring the quiet corners of Gozo, access to which would seriously endanger the suspension of any hired car, you can't beat the Jeep Safari. On this trip you bump over salt pans, scale up the roughest terrain and reach the highest point on Gozo for a

The rare pleasures of solitude on Gozo's sandy Ramla Bay

Setting off on a jeep safari to explore rural northern Gozo

wonderful panorama of the island.

The day is a long one, starting at 6.30am if you are staying in the Sliema area. This ensures an entire day on Gozo. The ferry crossing takes 20 to 25 minutes and there is no stopping at the busy harbour of Mġarr. You head straight for quiet countryside around Qala, taking rough tracks through fields and admiring the views across clumps of prickly pears to the island of Comino.

On the north of the island you drive along valleys of bamboo and pine, and stop for a dip at a tiny secluded cove or the sweeping sands of Ramla Bay. Near Marsalforn (a tourist resort which you bypass) the jeeps head for the salt pans and drive along the sandstone rocks, skirting shimmering blue seas.

Lunch is thoroughly Gozitan, well away from the crowds and washed down with limitless quantities of the potent local wine. Afternoons are spent exploring the fascinating west coast, where there is time to swim in the shallow waters of the Inland Sea, watch the fishermen or merely sit and admire the beauty of the seascape.

The last port of call is the pretty harbour of Xlendi. Then it's back to the ferry and – after a day in peaceful, rural Gozo – the seemingly cosmopolitan atmosphere of Malta.

Captain Morgan Tours, Dolphin Court, Tignè Seafront, Sliema. Tel: 331961; reservations can also be made through hotels and travel agents.

Comino may lack the usual tourist 'musts', but it still draws the crowds in summer

COMINO

Lying between Malta and Gozo, Comino is the smallest inhabited island of the Maltese archipelago. There are no cars, no highrise buildings, no hunters – just a couple of hotels, a tiny hamlet, a chapel, a disused cemetery, a police station, a piggery and a small chapel where mass is celebrated once a week. The only vehicles on the island are the Comino Hotel's Range Rover and a truck for transporting goods.

The permanent population of the island amounts to the grand total of three: an old lady and her two nephews (the policeman and the soldier at the tower work on a rota basis and are not resident on the island). In summer, however, the numbers are swollen by the staff who work in the two hotels, most of them commuting from Gozo, and the visitors who come in cruisers to the Blue Lagoon or stay for the day at the 4-star Comino Hotel.

The island itself is just a bare rock with the odd patch of *maquis* vegetation, along with a few mimosas and pines. The name Comino comes from the herbal plant cumin, which used to grow here in abundance. The island has now been made into a bird sanctuary and the cliffs are home to small colonies of breeding seabirds.

Comino has no sandy beaches but it is surrounded by glorious ultramarine waters and its caves and creeks are ideal for swimming, snorkelling and diving. The irridescent waters of the Blue Lagoon, between Comino and the rocky islet of Cominotto, are irresistible – especially if you get here early in the day, before the cruisers and yachts arrive from Malta. The seabed here is covered with white sand which reflects the sunlight so that the waters take on a glorious turquoise hue.

Hotels

The focal point of the island is the 4-star Comino Hotel, which also owns the nearby Nautico hotel and apartment complex. The eight boats that transport passengers from Malta and Gozo to Comino also belong to the hotel and many of the visitors who use them take lunch at the hotel and make the most of its facilities. So long as there are not too many other visitors with the same idea, the Comino Hotel makes a good base, located in an exotic spot with a beautiful pool right by the sea. There is a delightful sandy beach near by and a host of watersports facilities: sailing, windsurfing, water-skiing, snorkelling, boat trips, a diving school, canoes and paddle boats. There are also 10 tennis courts, with lessons available. Those who prefer their own company can take a picnic lunch and swim from one of the secluded spots off the rocks of Comino.

In winter the two hotels close down and your only way across to the island is by organised boat tours or by hiring the services of a fisherman. Comino is a good spot for a quiet walk at this time of year but remember to go equipped with food and drink. The best viewpoint is the Comino Tower, built in 1618 by Grand Master Wignacourt to protect the Gozo Channel from marauders. You can walk across the rickety drawbridge and around the parapets. Apart from the derelict isolation hospital near by, the only other real landmark (hotels apart) is the piggery; this was set up to restock farms on Malta after an outbreak of African swine-fever in 1980.

In season boats depart for Comino from Ċirkewwa on Malta seven times a day from 7.30am to 7pm. The trip takes about 25 minutes. There is also a regular seasonal service from Gozo. Information from Comino Hotel, Island of Comino. Tel: 529821.
Open: end of March to early November. Those wanting lunch at the hotel should make a reservation 24 hours in advance.

The irridescent waters of the Blue Lagoon, ideal for snorkelling

CAPTAIN MORGAN SUBMARINE

Billed as the 'Underwater Adventure of a Lifetime', the Captain Morgan submarine takes you down to explore the depths of the Mediterranean. Like the same firm's Jeep Safari (see page 142), this is an expensive treat, but it is certainly an exciting one. It is also very safe and is suitable for all ages.

Weather permitting, the submarine departs from Ċirkewwa, by the ferry landing stage every day, on the hour, from 10am until 4pm. The 26-seat craft comes from Finland and is fitted with all the latest gear; the seats are reasonably comfortable and the port-holes ensure good views of the underwater cliffs, caves, corals and marine life.

Look out for gurnards below

The main dive site is a 50m-long ocean tug, deliberately sunk for divers. The submarine dives to a depth of 30m to explore the wreck. The fish-feeding system on the submarine ensures a variety of sealife, including amberjack, tuna, moray eels, grouper, octopus and even the occasional diver who might be spotted snooping around the wreck or coming to wave at the windows of the submarine. The underwater flora is not spectacular but there are 17 different species of sponge to spot. After 20 minutes at the dive site, the submarine follows the sea bottom back to the cliffs before surfacing at the Ċirkewwa quay.
Captain Morgan, Dolphin Court, Tignè Seafront, Sliema. Tel: 331961.
Reservations can also be made through hotels and travel agents.

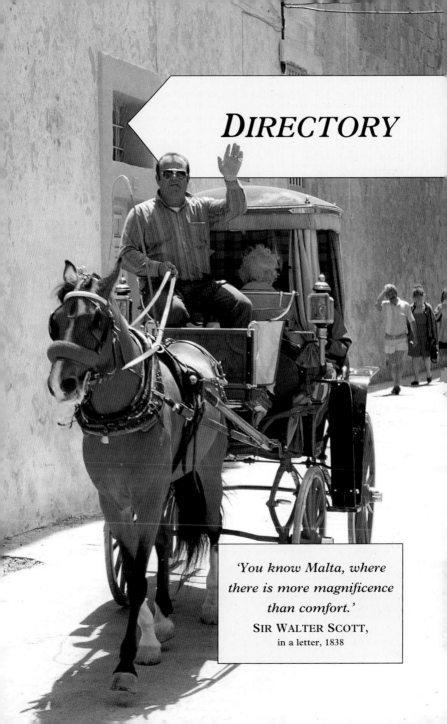

DIRECTORY

'You know Malta, where there is more magnificence than comfort.'
SIR WALTER SCOTT,
in a letter, 1838

Shopping

Malta could never be described as a great shopping centre, and many Maltese go on a day trip to Sicily when they want a shopping spree. The best buys for visitors are the local crafts, which are all conveniently displayed and demonstrated in craft villages on Malta and Gozo. Crafts aside, the best shopping is in Triq ir-Repubblika (Republic Street), Valletta.

Department stores and clothes shops are uninspiring compared to their mainland European counterparts and the prices in international shops, such as Marks & Spencer, Benetton and Next are substantially higher.

The best locations to experience the bustle of Maltese life are the Sunday markets in Valletta and Marsaxlokk.

CRAFT VILLAGES
Generally speaking the best places to see – and the cheapest places to buy – local handicrafts are the two crafts villages on Malta and on Gozo.

Ta'Qali Craft Centre, Ta'Qali
Authentic Maltese crafts are displayed on the site of a World War II aerodrome. Here you can watch working silver-

smiths, glassblowers, potters, ironsmiths, stonecarvers, lacemakers and jewellers. A visit to the village features on day tours of the island but it is more satsifying to go independently and browse (and buy) at your own leisure.
For full details, see page 78.

Ta'Dbieġi Crafts Village
This is Gozo's version of the Ta'Qali Craft Centre, displaying and selling local crafts, but all on a smaller scale.
On the road between San Lawrenz and Għarb, Gozo. Tel: 562316 for information.

WHAT TO BUY
Brass and iron
Brass dolphin door-knockers, imitating those of Mdina and other old quarters, are favourite souvenirs. Wrought ironwork is a traditional Maltese skill and items range from candlesticks to an entire suit of armour.

Ceramics
Local pottery is not as varied as you might expect from a Mediterranean island. The styles are mainly rustic and the predominant colours are brown and blue. Very reasonably priced are the ceramic and sculpture 'seconds' sold at the Craft Centre in Ta'Qali.

Glass
Local glassware is arguably the island's best buy. It is stylish, beautifully coloured

Maltese glass is stylish and good value

Watch weavers at work before buying handmade bedspreads

and reasonably priced. Vases, pots and ornaments come in various shades of blue and green, often in a mottled effect. For displays of glass-blowing and an excellent selection try **Mdina Glass**, Ta'Qali Craft Centre (tel: 415786); Gozo Glass, San Lawrenz, Gozo (tel: 560354).

Jewellery

The Maltese have been making jewellery for centuries and the island is full of silversmiths and goldsmiths. Many specialise in gold and silver filigree. The streets of Valletta have the best choice.

Leather

Leather shops abound, especially shoe shops, though the quality is not the same as that to be found in Italy. You can watch leather goods being made at the two crafts villages or use the 3-day made-to-measure service offered by **The Leather Shop**, Triq Bisazza (Bisazza Street), Sliema (tel: 316618), also at 12 Triq Nofs-in-Nhar (South Street), Valletta (tel: 220427).

Textiles

Malta's textile industry goes back centuries. Today most of the authentic handmade items you will see are made on Gozo. Beware, however, of imitation lace. Among the range of genuine items are lace-edged handkerchiefs, napkins, tablecloths and full-lace shawls. For the best choice try the crafts village of Ta'Dbieġi, the shops behind It-Tokk square in Victoria or the shops of Xlendi.

Equally abundant are the cheap and chunky woollen cardigans and sweaters that hang outside the shops in Malta and Gozo. Cotton goods such as T-shirts, towels and jeans are very reasonably priced, especially those sold in the markets.

Malta Weave is an especially hardwearing cloth that is used for making dresses, skirts and bedspreads. You can watch weaving displays and buy from: **Carrie Attard**, 20a Triq Sant Agata (St Agatha Street), Rabat (almost opposite St Paul's Catacombs). Tel: 454311.

Entertainment

*M*alta is essentially a peaceful island, where nightlife, even in the capital, amounts to no more than a drink or two in a bar or an evening trot in a horse-drawn *karrozzin* round the city's floodlit ramparts.

Those seeking late-night action should head northwest to the small area of St Julian's known as Paceville. Here you will find scores of discos, pubs, late-night bars, live music and Malta's one and only nightclub. In summer the neon-lit streets are crammed with action-seekers. St Julian's is also home to Malta's casino – the only place where the nightlife could be described as glitzy. Lesser concentrations of bars with live music, and the occasional discos, can be found in Sliema and in the St Paul's area, around Buġibba and Qawra.

Cocktails and gaming chips at the Dragonara Palace Casino

Discos open early in the evening for the benefit of the young (and not-so-young) Maltese visiting from the countryside who have to catch the last bus home at around 9pm. For the rest, the music throbs on into the early hours of the morning.

The older generation of visitors to Malta are usually quite content with hotel entertainment, which takes the form of folk nights, cabarets and possibly discos. These events are normally open to non-residents.

On the cultural side, Malta has several English-language theatres and cinemas. The delightful Manoel Theatre (see page 153) puts on ballet, opera and

concert performances in addition to plays. One of the most important cultural events in the Maltese calendar is Maltafest – a month of concerts, recitals, jazz performances, open-air theatre and art exhibitions – which takes place from mid-July to mid-August.

What's On!

The best sources of information on entertainment are the local newspapers and the fortnightly publication *What's On in Malta and Gozo*, sold at souvenir and book shops. The Malta National Tourism Organisation (see **Tourist Offices**, page 189) publishes an events calendar, detailing regular and one-off events.

CASINO

An ornate classical mansion on Dragonara Point, built in the 1830s, forms the elegant setting for the island's casino. Formerly this was only open to non-Maltese but now anyone can lay their bets – provided that they are dressed correctly and pay the entrance fee. Rough-looking bouncers see to the rest. The Maltese have an obsession with gambling and, when they are not in the casino, the chances are they will be trying their luck at a bingo party or buying tickets from one of the island's ubiquitous lottery offices.

Dragonara Palace.Casino, Dragonara Point, St Julian's. Tel: 312888. Open: Monday to Saturday 8pm–4am. Jacket and tie compulsory.

CINEMA

Cinema has inevitably given way to TV and videos (until copyright laws began to be enforced in 1993, pirated videos sold for a song). The following cinemas show English-language films:

Malta's cinemas show the latest movies

The Ambassador, Gawhra, Gojjell and **Embassy** (all four in one complex), Triq Santa Lucija (St Lucia Street), Valletta. Tel: 220549.

The Alhambra, Triq it-Torri (Tower Road), Sliema. Tel: 313463.

The Golden Knight International Amateur Film and Video Festival, popular with local and foreign film enthusiasts, is organised by the Malta Amateur Cine Circle and takes place in the latter part of November.

CONCERTS

The Manoel Symphony Orchestra performs at the Manoel Theatre (see page 153). Classical concerts are also held in St John's Co-Cathedral in Valletta. In summer there are occasional concerts in the San Anton Gardens in Attard (see page 75) and the Buskett Gardens near Mdina (see page 69).

Concerts, vocal recitals, choral and ballet presentations are organised by the Malta Cultural Institute at the Casino Maltese in Valletta from January to June and from October to December.

The International Choir Festival, held in the third week of November, sees performances by choirs from all over Europe.

Dancing, modern style, at Styx II disco

DISCOTHEQUES – MALTA
Acsis
Large, stylish disco with high-tec laser show.
Triq San Ġorġ (St George's Road), St Julian's. Tel: 318078. Open: 7pm–4am. Admission charge.
Beachaven
One of the few discos right on the coast, with views of the bay.
It-Telgha Tax Xemxija (Xemxija Hill), St Paul's Bay. Tel: 573682. Open: 9pm–4am. Admission charge.
Dewdrops
Disco attracting the twenty- to thirty-year olds. Mid-evening show.
Triq Ball (Ball Street), Paceville. Open: 9.30pm–2am. Admission charge.
Styx II
Similar to Acsis (see above), with competing laser lighting, plus video wall.

St George's Bay (below Eden Beach Hotel), St Julian's. Tel: 333434. Open: Monday to Thursday 9.30pm–2am, Friday to Saturday 7pm–4am. Admission charge.
Ta'Cassia
Not so much a disco as a farmhouse with live music and open-air dancing. An attractive, off-the-beaten-track location, where you can dine outside in summer and in converted stables in winter.
Triq Qawra (Qawra Road), Qawra. Tel: 571435. Open: 7pm–midnight. Free.
Vibes
A disco favoured by slightly older visitors, away from action-packed Paceville.
San Gwann, Sliema. Tel: 370028. Open: 9.30pm–2am. Admission charge.

DISCOTHEQUE – GOZO
La Grotta
Unique disco in a cave under the street, with open-air dancing in summer. The most attractive of all the discos on the islands, this draws many Maltese as well as Gozitans.
Triq Xlendi (Xlendi Road), Xlendi. Tel: 551149. Open: summers only from 9pm (no official closing time). Admission charge.

FOLK NIGHTS
Maltese folk dances are colourful affairs, with Arabic and Sicilian influences much in evidence. The performances laid on for visitors are not necessarily authentic in every respect, but the verve of the dancers ensures a lively and colourful evening. Many hotels organise occasional folk evenings, featuring local dancers.
Palazzo Pescatore
This old mansion, converted to a fish restaurant, puts on special folk evenings once a week.
Triq San Pawl (St Paul's Street), St Paul's Bay. Tel: 573182.

NIGHTCLUB
The Eden Palladium
This is Malta's one and only nightclub. An evening here consists of live music, a laser show and a variety of rather mediocre cabaret acts performed by magicians, comedians, dancers and singers. There is no shortage of refreshment, with five bars and a substantial pre-show buffet dinner.
St George's Bay, St Julian's. Tel: 319899/341191. Open: Tuesday to Friday from 8.30pm, Saturday and Sunday from 10.15pm. Admission charge.

NIGHT EXCURSION
Captain Morgan's Party Night at Sea
This cruise includes swimming and a barbeque dinner with plenty of wine, followed by dancing and games.
Captain Morgan Tours. Tel: 331961. Boats depart from Sliema Marina every Tuesday from May to October.

THEATRE, BALLET AND OPERA
The Manoel Theatre
Valletta's delightful Manoel Theatre is Malta's main venue for music, dance and drama. Plays, opera, concerts, recitals and ballet performances take place all year round but the main season lasts from October to May. The theatre alone is worth a visit (see page 36). It is one of the oldest in Europe, with a magnificent gilded ceiling and tiers of ornate boxes. Recently the theatre's 260th anniversary was celebrated with a gala performance of *La Traviata*. Another glittering performance was the concert by the Manoel Theatre Orchestra put on for the visit of Queen Elizabeth and the Duke of Edinburgh in May 1992.

Both local and foreign artists perform at the theatre and there are occasional visits from world-famous pianists, singers and actors. Plays are only occasionally performed in English. The theatre provides free brochures detailing the season's cultural events. One of the regular highlights is the traditional pantomime, performed at Christmas.
118 Triq it-Teatru il-Qadim (Old Theatre Street), Valletta. Box office – tel: 246389.

Astra Theatre
Built in the 1960s as a theatre, the Astra has been used principally as an opera house for the last 15 years. For financial reasons it also doubles as a cinema.
Triq ir-Repubblika (Republic Street), Victoria, Gozo. Tel: 556256.

Aurora Theatre
This rival to the Astra also acts as an opera house, theatre and cinema.
Centru Parrokjali Katidral, Triq ir-Repubblika (Republic Street), Victoria, Gozo. Tel: 556452/556974.

A more traditional style of dance

Festivals

*G*iven the Maltese passion for *festas* and pageantry, it is not surprising that almost every parish celebrates the feast day of its local patron saint. These festivities last several days and consist of colourful parades accompanied by brass bands and spectacular fireworks displays. The final day of the *festa* sees the life-size statue of the patron saint carried out of the church and through the village streets.

To witness a local festival it is best to visit Malta between May and October when the majority take place. Those *festas* that do not occur on a public holiday are celebrated on the weekend before or after the saint's feast day.

Feast of St Paul's Shipwreck

10 February, Valletta
This commemorates the shipwreck of St Paul on Malta in AD60 and is one of Malta's major *festas*. As the carved wooden statue of St Paul is carried out of the church of St Paul's Shipwreck, hundreds of pigeons are let loose and petards (small cannons) are fired over rooftops.

Carnival

Three days before Ash Wednesday
Carnival, celebrating the end of winter and arrival of spring, was first staged on Malta in the 16th century but then went into decline when the Knights departed. The jollifications have now been reinstated, primarily as a tourist event. Carnival in Malta may not rank with Venice or Rio but it is a colourful affair, with whole towns and villages becoming the stage sets for exotic parades, carnival floats, folk-dancing contests and firework displays. One of the few places where the locals really let their hair down is Nadur in Gozo. The big events, however, are held in Valletta.

Easter

The run up to Easter is typified by solemn religious processions. On Good Friday hooded *penitentes* carry life-size statues through the streets depicting scenes from the Passion and Crucifixion of Christ. Easter Sunday sees somewhat merrier processions, with statues of 'The Risen Christ' being carried through the towns and villages. Those of Vittoriosa and Cospicua are among the best.

Freedom Day

31 March
This national holiday celebrates the final withdrawal of British forces from Malta in 1979. Firework displays and parades take place in Valletta and Vittoriosa, while commemorative celebrations are held at the War Memorial in Floriana.

St Peter and St Paul

29 June
Known as *Imnarja*, this major festival, originally a harvest festival, is held in Buskett Gardens near Mdina (see pages 72–3).

St George

Late July
The climax of this *festa* is the horse racing that takes place in Republic Street (once called Racecourse Street) in Victoria on Gozo.

Preparing for the Festival of Our Lady of Lourdes in the village of Qrendi

Feast of the Assumption
15 August
Statues of the Virgin are carried through the streets in many towns and villages.

Our Lady of Victories
8 September
The best known of all the Maltese *festas*, this one marks the defeat of the Turks at the end of the Great Siege of 1565; it also coincides with the end of the Blitz of Malta in 1942 and with the Feast of the Birth of the Virgin. A *festa* is held in the majority of parishes, while the highlight is the Regatta held in the Grand Harbour.

Independence Day
21 September
Celebrations throughout Malta mark the day in 1964 when Malta attained its independence.

International Choir Festival
Third week in November
Choirs from all over Europe take part in this festival, organised by the Ministry of Tourism.

Feast of the Immaculate Conception
8 December
This *festa* is celebrated everywhere, but the most colourful events take place in Cospicua.

Republic Day
13 December
Processions, music and fireworks in Vittoriosa commemorate the day in 1974 when Malta was declared a republic.

Children

*T*he Maltese love children and welcome them with the warmth and enthusiasm you might expect of a Mediterranean people. Malta may not be the obvious choice for a bucket-and-spade holiday (sandy beaches are scarce), nor are there many theme parks; the island does, however, offer dozens of playgrounds, an abundance of cafés serving sausages and chips, sunshine for most of the year and sparkling blue waters for swimming and boat trips.

BOAT TRIPS AND CRUISES

The traditional harbour cruise (see pages 44–5) takes in historical forts, battlements and creeks and provides entertainment for all ages. Alternatively you can take boat tours around Malta or Gozo, cruising alongside caves, grottoes and salt pans, and stopping for a dip and buffet lunch in one of the bays. The day

Street football Maltese style

trip to Gozo or Comino takes in a dip in the glorious Blue Lagoon, where the shallow clear waters and the sandy bed make for excellent swimming. However, the trip which normally provides the most excitement for the younger (and older) generation is the Captain Morgan submarine trip, from Ċirkewwa on Malta (see page 146). For a fraction of the price, the Underwater Safari boat trip from Buġibba provides plenty of fun as you peer through underwater windows at fishes, marine flora and sponges (see page 114).

All the above trips are organized by Captain Morgan Cruises, Dolphin Court, Tignè Seafront, Sliema, Malta. Tel: 331961. Tickets for tours can be purchased in advance from hotels, travel agents and numerous outlets throughout the islands. Pick-ups can normally be arranged from hotels. Discounts of up to 30 per cent are offered for children.

CHILDREN'S ATTRACTIONS
Popeye Village

Children naturally enjoy the film set of *Popeye* (see page 111) at Anchor Bay. The village can be reached on horseback from Golden Bay.

San Anton Gardens

The gardens of the San Anton Palace in Attard have a miniscule zoo and dozens of cats (see page 75).

Splash and Fun Park
Malta's only leisure park provides water-chutes, bouncy castles and a playground with dinosaurs (see page 115).

HOTELS AND SELF-CATERING
The few hotels with sandy beaches (among them Ramla Bay, Paradise Bay, Golden Sands) provide children's facilities but are out on a limb from the main centres. Unless you are happy to stay put or visit the island's other sights by organised tour, a hired car is crucial.

Many of the large self-catering complexes (or 'aparthotels') in St Julian's Bay or Buġibba also offer a range of children's facilities. Prices drop dramatically off-season both in self-catering and hotel accommodation, with some establishments offering free child places among their incentives.

Accommodation in Gozo offers less in the way of children's facilities but there is a very friendly relaxed atmosphere about the island and children will love the ferry crossing from Malta.

MUSEUMS AND CULTURE
There are no museums specifically geared to children. For nature lovers the Museum of Natural History in Mdina (see page 65) has displays of local birds, fish, mammals and shells. Very small children should not visit the neighbouring Mdina Dungeons (see page 64), though older children will love the gruesome scenes of death and torture.

The two multivision shows (the Malta Experience, page 36 and the Mdina Experience, page 65) are sufficiently lively and spectacular for children of around seven and upwards to enjoy. The Gozo Heritage (see page 130), recreating scenes from the island's history, is also suitable for children.

Having fun beside the sea

SWIMMING AND SPORTS
For children who are able to swim there is excellent bathing from rocks or concrete lidos. Rowing boats and pedaloes can be hired from most of the main bays. Tuition is available in water-skiing and windsurfing, and from Golden Bay and Mellieħa Bay children can enjoy a high-speed trip on an inflatable 'sea-sausage'.

For the older and teenage group, Paceville (St Julian's) provides a bowling centre and a cluster of lively discos.

Sport

*S*ports enthusiasts are spoilt for choice on Malta. The climate and clear waters make for excellent watersports and some of the best diving in the Mediterranean. Many large hotels have their own sporting or recreational facilities, and if not there are several sports clubs to choose from, including the Marsa Sports Club, the island's principal sporting venue.

MARSA SPORTS CLUB

This huge sporting complex has sufficient facilities to keep you active for days. Affordable membership is available on a daily or weekly basis. Facilities include an 18-hole golf course, 18 hard tennis courts, five squash courts, an 18-hole mini golf course, a cricket pitch and billiards tables. In addition there is a fitness centre with gym and sauna and, in season, a swimming pool. In the vicinity of the club there are polo grounds, a horse-racing track, plus football and rubgy pitches.

4km south of Valletta, on the outskirts of Marsa. Tel: 233851.

WATERSPORTS
DIVING

Malta and Gozo are ideal for diving (see pages 162–3) and the costs are reasonable by European standards. A full range of PADI (Professional Association of Diving Instructors) and BSAC (British Sub-Aqua Club) courses is offered, as well as taster sessions for the total beginner.

Diving takes place either from the shore or from boats. For any diving course you need a medical certificate of physical fitness. This can be arranged locally for a fee (sometimes the fee is included in the price of a course).

The Maltese National Tourism Organisation (see **Tourist Offices**, page 189) provides excellent leaflets on diving courses, diving clubs, equipment hire, emergency numbers, and information on the best dive sites on the islands. All necessary equipment can be hired on the spot. Any experienced diver wishing to dive independently of a diving school must obtain a Malta Government Dive Permit or present a certificate to the authorities equivalent to at least the CMAS (Confederation Mondial des Activities Subaquatiques) 2-star certificate.

The following are reliable licensed diving schools:

Calypso Diving Centre, Calypso Hotel, Marsalforn, Gozo. Tel: 562020.

Diveshack, 14a Qui-Si-Sana Place, Sliema. Tel: 320594.

Divewise Services, Dragonara Complex, St Julian's. Tel: 336441.

Frankie's Gozo Diving Centre, Triq Mġarr (Mġarr Road), Xewkija, Gozo. Tel: 551315/555835.

Maltaqua, Triton Court, Triq il-Mosta (Mosta Road), St Paul's Bay. Tel: 571873.

St Andrew's Divers Cove, St Simon Street, Xlendi Bay, Gozo. Tel: 551301.

FISHING

No fishing licence is required and fishing is permitted from the rocks anywhere around the islands. It is possible to go out to sea if you arrange it with a local fisherman, but you are likely to pay a great deal for the privilege. Ask at the village of Marsaxlokk and be prepared to bargain.

SAILING AND YACHTING

Regattas are held from April to November, many of them starting from the Royal Malta Yacht Club. The main races are the Comino Regatta in June, the Malta to Syracuse (Sicily) race for keelboats in July and the Rimini/Malta/Rimini race in August.

Malta has exceptionally good boating facilities. The main yachting centre focuses on Msida Marina, one of the best-equipped marinas in the Mediterranean. It provides 870 berths, with facilities such as electricity, water, showers, IDD telephones and 24-hour security. The Mġarr Yachting Centre in Gozo now has 120 berths.

For advice on chartering yachts and for details of local and international competitions contact: **The Royal Malta Yacht Club**, Couvre Porte, Fort Manoel, Manoel Island (tel: 331131/333109).

SNORKELLING

The clear Maltese waters are excellent for snorkelling. Equipment can be bought or hired locally.

WATERPOLO

The Maltese are mad about waterpolo and special pools have been constructed in some of the main centres. The national pitch is at Marsaskala.

WATERSKIING

Facilities are available on the main beaches. The most popular are to be found at Malta's Mellieħa beach and Golden Bay. Waterskiing trips and tuition are available from **Divewise Services**, Dragonara Complex,

Determined to get a catch – fishing is possible all year round in Malta

St Julian's (tel: 336441).

WINDSURFING

Windsurfing boards can be hired at the main beaches in Malta. Mellieħa is particularly good.

The Sicily-Malta Windsurfing Race, held in May, and the International Open Class Boardsailing Championships, held in September, both attract competitors at international level.

LANDSPORTS

ARCHERY

The Sagittarius Archery Club (tel: 338860) organises archery at the Marsa Sports Club (see page 158). The International Archery tournament takes place mid-April each year in the club grounds.

ATHLETICS

The first Malta Marathon, held in February 1986, proved an instant success. Since then it has become an established event, held every February. The route is 42km, from Mdina to Sliema. A ladies half-marathon is run concurrently. The Malta Amateur Athletic Association organises track and field events, culminating in the athletics championships held in May at the Marsa Stadium.

BOWLING

The **Eden Super Bowl**, St George's Bay, St Julian's (tel: 319888/341196) has 20 tenpin bowling alleys and fully

Putting for the hole at Marsa Sports Club

computerised scoring. The Malta Tenpin Bowling Association organises various tournaments and championships here.

The **Msida Bowling Centre,** Enrico Mizzi Street, Msida (tel: 313424) has bowling alleys, plus pool tables and video games.

The Maltese *bocci* (akin to the French *petanque*) is very popular at village level. The *bocci* league and competitions are played mainly between April and October.

FOOTBALL

The Maltese are crazy about soccer and there are countless teams on the islands. The regular football season is from September to May. Malta competes at an international level and the main venue for matches is the National Stadium at Ta'Qali.

The local Football Assocation headquarters is in Valletta at 280 Triq San Pawl (St Paul Street) (tel: 222697).

GOLF

The only golf course on Malta is the 18-hole course at the Marsa Sports Club (see page 158).

HORSE-RACING

This is one of Malta's top spectator sports and on Sunday afternoons the Marsa Racecourse draws large crowds. Programmes normally consist of seven or eight trotting races and one flat race. For the times of races look in the local papers. For information on horse-racing, tel: 224800 (Marsa Racing Club).

RIDING

Riding and lessons are available at the following schools:
Darmanin Riding School, 15 Stables Lane, Marsa (tel: 235649 or 228507).

Trotting races take place every Sunday at Marsa Racecourse

Golden Sands Hotel Riding School,
Golden Bay (tel: 573961).
**Mellieħa Holiday Centre Riding
School**, Mellieħa Bay, (tel: 573901).
Santa Cassia Riding School, c/o
Ta'Cassia Restaurant, Qawra, St Paul's
Bay (tel: 471435).

SHOOTING
Sadly, one of the favourite Maltese sports
is shooting or trapping anything that
flies. Unlike the French who will make a
meal (or at least a pâté) out of a small
songbird, the Maltese normally kill for
the sport or trap birds to sell in cages.
The sounds of gunshots, and the sight of
spent cartridges on paths and lanes, are
all too familiar. The local Ornithological
Society estimates that over a million
finches are trapped, and around 200,000
thrushes shot, every year.

A heart-rending sight (especially in
spring and autumn) are the small birds in
tiny cages, set out in rows to lure others
of the same species. Near by you can

usually spot a trapper peeping out of his
stone hide, ready to shoot or activate the
mist net. As a visitor you are advised not
to interfere or even take photographs –
some trappers don't have a licence and
may get angry. Although recent
legislation gives some protection to
certain species of birds, in particular
migratory ones, the law is rarely
enforced. After all, there are 30,000
hunters on Malta, which means that any
political party determined to enforce the
laws would face the loss of a lot of votes.

TENNIS AND SQUASH
Some hotels have their own courts and
there are excellent facilities for tennis and
squash players at the Marsa Sports Club
(see page 158). The following clubs also
have tennis and squash courts:
The Mistra Sports Centre, Mistra
Village, St Paul's Bay (tel: 580481).
The Calypso Sports Complex,
Calypso Hotel, Marsalforn Bay, Gozo
(tel: 562000).

PLUMBING THE DEPTHS

Quite justifiably Malta calls itself 'a Mecca for Divers'. The clarity and depth of water, the spectacular underwater scenery and the mild sea temperatures combine to make the Maltese archipelago one of the best spots in the Mediterranean for diving and snorkelling.

Exotic tropical fish are unlikely to cross your path and big game, such as shark and tuna, are rarely ever seen near the coast (the 9m-long white shark found dead in a net in Maltese waters in 1987 was something of a freak given that white sharks don't inhabit the Mediterranean). Species that can be seen, lurking in the caves and grottoes of the coastline, are groupers (weighing up to 70kg), amberjack, bream, flying gurnard, squid and large octopus. Species to steer clear of – beautiful though they may look – are the scorpion fish and the stingray.

Thanks to the predominantly rocky coast of the islands and the scarcity of sandy beaches, the waters are free of any serious pollution and the visibility on average is up to 30m. Such conditions have encouraged underwater photography in a big way and led to

major competitions, drawing experts from all over the world.

Divers plunge the depths all year round. Even in a severe winter the sea temperature never drops below 13°C and in summer it is warm enough to dive without a wetsuit.

Two shipwrecks, one a British World War II destroyer in Marsamxett Harbour and another, a deliberately sunk ocean tug near Ċirkewwa, have opened up whole new dimensions for divers.

Malta provides excellent facilities for divers of all standards. Diving clubs organise day trips to Gozo and Comino, where some of the best diving sites are located; some also organise night dives.

Diving clubs on the islands are well equipped and standards of safety are high – whether you're doing your first dive off the seashore at Sliema or plunging 40m to the boulder-strewn depths of the Mediterranean.

The facilities for divers are excellent on Malta and the visibility is outstanding; the attractions include sunken wrecks and varied marine life

Food and Drink

Food in Malta may not rank as gourmet cuisine, but it's very reasonably priced and there are plenty of places to choose from. Beyond the proliferation of pizzerias, pasta houses and snackbars, there are occasional gourmet restaurants and a good range of places serving fresh fish. The latter can be anything from family-run seaside cafés to fully fledged restaurants which entice you in with their tanks full of live lobsters.

FOOD

Menus are almost always translated into English. The following are a few of the local dishes which you may come across if you happen to eat in restaurants serving Maltese cuisine.

Soups

Aljotta fish soup seasoned with onions and herbs.

Brodu basic soup made from boiled beef and flavoured with celery, marrow and turnip.

Kawlata vegetable soup with added pork or Maltese sausages.

Octopus is cooked with wine and garlic

Minestra vegetable soup, similar to minestrone but thicker.

Pasta

Ravjul Maltese ravioli, stuffed with ricotta cheese.

Timpana macaroni layered with meat, vegetables, cheese and eggs, baked in pastry.

Vegetables

Locally-grown vegetables are often served with a stuffing made of minced meat, onions, parsley, olives, breadcrumbs, herbs and tomato purée.

Brungiel stuffed aubergines.

Qaqoċċ mimli stuffed globe artichokes.

Qara'bali mimli stuffed marrow.

Fish

Fresh fish is expensive and not always available, especially in winter. 'Fresh' on a menu may merely mean that the fish was frozen as soon as it was caught.

Acciola amberjack.

Calamari squid (stuffed, fried or braised).

Cerna grouper.

Dott stone bass.

Fanfru pilot fish (a member of the mackerel family).

Granċ crab.

Merluzzo red mullet.

Pixxispad swordfish.

Qarnita octopus (often fried in garlic

or braised in red-wine sauce).
Tunnagg tuna, often cooked with
tomatoes, green peppers and onions.

Meat
Braġioli slices of beef rolled round a
mixture of minced meat, olives, egg,
bacon, breadcrumbs and parsley.
Fenek biz-Zalza rabbit stew, made with
onions, herbs and wine.
Torta tal-fenek rabbit pie.

Cheese
Ġbejna sheep's milk cheese, served
either fresh, half-dried or peppered. A
speciality of Gozo, this comes in small
rounds and is excellent with the local
bread and tomatoes.

Bread
Maltese bread (*hobz*) is very crusty on
the outside and soft inside. According to
a national newspaper survey the average
daily consumption is a kilo of bread per
person! If you taste the real thing, made
by traditional methods (as still used in
Qormi) you will probably understand
why.

CAFÉS, KIOSKS AND SNACKBARS

Tea and coffee (which varies from weak
instant coffee to excellent *espresso*) is
served everywhere and the prices, even in
a pavement café on a square in central
Valletta, are reasonable by European
standards.

Another source of snacks are the
roadside kiosks, selling sandwiches,
pastries, nuts, cakes, macaroons and
other sundries to satisfy the sweet
Maltese tooth. The best bet are the
pastizzi rikotta – small triangles of puff
pastry filled with ricotta cheese and
served hot.

Maltese bread is well worth sampling

DRINK

The general rule of thumb is to avoid the
very cheapest local wines. Move up a
couple of price brackets (which will still
work out far cheaper than choosing an
imported Italian brand) and you may be
pleasantly surprised. Safe bets are the
following wines from the Marsovin
range: La Valette, Merlot Noir and
Cabernet Sauvignon (reds), Verdala
(white and rosé), Pinot Grigio and
Chardonnay (whites). Less palatable are
the Marsovin Special Reserve wines,
especially the red, and any of the
Lachryma Vitis wines. Be very wary of
the strong Gozitan wines – 14° is not
uncommon though the alcoholic content
is rarely shown on the bottle. Many
restaurant owners make their own wine
or have it made specially for them. It is
certainly worth trying, though you may
end up (like some of the locals) adding
7-Up to disguise the taste!

The local soft drink is *Kinnie*, a bitter-
sweet aromatic drink made from herbs.
Farson's Blue Label and Hopleaf lagers,
made from British hops and drunk for
years by British servicemen, are
excellent.

MALTESE REGIONAL

High standards of cuisine were introduced to Malta by the Knights. Food came high on the list of priorities for this supposedly monastic and frugal order. To serve their tastes, chefs were brought in from abroad, wine flowed in from France and ice was imported from the snowy peak of Mount Etna, on Sicily.

Foreign influences still play a major role in Maltese cuisine. The island's close proximity to Italy has inevitably determined its favourite dish of pasta; the British left their mark in the form of roast beef and apple pie, fish and chips.

The real local dishes, however, have the unmistakable stamp of the Mediterranean. Essential ingredients are the local herbs and vegetables, such as sun-ripened tomatoes, green peppers, marrows, aubergines and artichokes. Made into bulky Maltese soups, and eaten with the local crusty bread, these make a more than adequate meal.

Fish is abundant and comes steamed, braised or grilled. Choose from sea bream, swordfish, grouper, tuna, pilot fish, amberjack, prawns, lobsters – and many more. Autumn brings the *lampuka*, a fish that breeds near the Nile Delta and swarms around the Maltese coast in September and October. The somewhat enigmatic taste has been compared to cod,

CUISINE

mackerel and whitebait! It is perhaps best tasted in the form of *lampuka* pie, cooked with tomatoes, onions, parsley, peas and cauliflower, then encased in crispy pastry.

Among Malta's few regional meat dishes is *braġioli*, similar to beef olives, made with thin slices of beef wrapped round a minced meat, egg and bacon stuffing. Done well it is delicious.

A favourite and long-established Maltese dish is rabbit. This is served in a variety of forms, which you can taste by going out for a traditional *fenkata* (or 'rabbit evening'). This starts with spaghetti in rabbit sauce, followed by fried rabbit or rabbit stew (complete with liver and kidneys); the meal ends with nuts and figs. Ideally you should experience this in a basic country bar full of villagers and wash it down with lots of local wine. The village of Mġarr on Malta is the place to try it.

Traditional Maltese food ranges from fresh fish and rabbit stew to tasty parcels of pastry filled with cheese

Restaurants

*T*he majority of Malta's restaurants serve Italian food and range from basic pasta houses to 4-star restaurants. In addition there are pubs and cafés serving typical British fare, a smattering of ethnic restaurants (particularly in St Julian's), a small handful of top-notch French restaurants and a multitude of fast-food outlets. Simple local village bars, often a stone's throw from the village church, can produce some surprisingly wholesome meals at rock-bottom prices.

Most restaurants close for one day a week and some shut in mid-winter. Lunch is served from noon to 2.30 or 3pm but not all restaurants open at midday. Evening meals are served from 6 or 7pm to 9.30 or 10.30pm. Many snack bars and pizzerias are open all day.

In the list of recommended restaurants, the price symbol indicates the approximate cost per person of a three-course meal excluding drinks, but including tax, cover charge and the 10 per cent service charge. For simpler establishments, such as pizzerias, the price symbol indicates the cost of two, rather than three, courses. The price for fresh fish is frequently not shown on menus. Make sure to ask before you order.

£ Lm2.50–Lm5
££ Lm6–Lm8
£££ Lm9–Lm11
££££ Lm12–Lm15
Add Lm1.70 for a bottle of palatable local wine.

MALTA
BIRŻEBBUĠA
Al Fresco £
Geared specifically to children: puzzles, pizzas and pasta.
St George's Bay. Tel: 681422. Overlooking the bay.

DINGLI
Bobbyland £
Spectacular views over Dingli Cliffs.

Serves rabbit, duck and fish.
Panoramic Road, Dingli Cliffs. Tel: 452895.

MARSASKALA
Christopher's ££££
Small and exceptionally charming, with the best cuisine in town.
29 Triq ix-Xatt (Marina Street). Tel: 829142.
Fishermen's Restaurant ££
Unspectacular setting but crowds flock here for the fish.
St Thomas Bay. Tel: 822049.

MARSAXLOKK
Hunter's Tower ££££
Large fish restaurant with panoramic views over the bay.
Triq il-Wilga (Wilga Street). Tel: 871356.
Ir-Rizzu £
Excellent value for fish.
Xatt is-Sajjieda. Tel: 871569.
Pisces ££
Waterside fish restaurant with modern décor.
49/50 Xatt is-Sajjieda. Tel: 684956.
Skuna II ££
Bustling family-run fish restaurant.
Duncan Street. Tel: 871575.

MDINA

Bacchus ££££
Beautiful old town house serving
elaborate Italian cuisine.
*Triq Inguanez (Inguanez Street).
Tel: 454981.*

Medina ££££
International cuisine and the ambience
of a lovely old 'Norman' house.
*7 Triq is-Salib Imqaddes (Holy Cross
Street). Tel: 454004.*

MELLIEĦA

The Arches ££££
Exceptionally elegant cuisine, with
surroundings to match.
*113 Triq il-Kbira (Main Street).
Tel: 573436.*

MĠARR

Friends to All £
Basic local bar, ideal for rabbit served
local style.
Triq il-Kbira (Main Street) Tel: 574605.

MOSTA

Ta'Marija £££
Authentic Maltese cuisine in a converted
farmhouse.
*Triq Constitution (Constitution Street).
Tel: 434444.*

ST JULIAN'S/PACEVILLE

Chains II £££
Small and stylish, overlooking Spinola
Bay.
*95 Triq G Borġ Olivier (Grenfell Street),
St Julian's. Tel: 331114.*

Barracuda ££££
Luxury, with lovely views. Brilliant
spaghetti with lobster sauce.
*194 Triq il-Kbira (Main Street),
St Julian's. Tel: 331817.*

Chicago Pizza Shack £
Part of a deep-pan pizza chain.

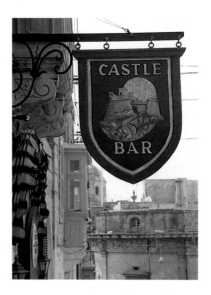

Cheerful and noisy, on Spinola Bay.
*Triq Spinola (Spinola Road), St Julian's.
Tel: 316943.*

Clouds £
Very popular fast-food outlet serving
pasta, pizza, burgers and homemade
desserts.
*Triq San Gorġ (St George's Road),
Paceville. Tel 319646.*

La Dolce Vita ££££
One of the best places to go for fresh
fish.
*159 Triq San Gorġ (St George's Road),
St Julian's. Tel: 337806.*

Hasta Luego ££
Mexican cuisine and décor; a good
choice of dishes for vegetarians.
*58a Triq il-Wilġa (Wilga Street), Paceville.
Tel: 333294.*

Kandles £
Small and intimate, serving Javanese
cuisine.
*Triq Paceville (Paceville Street), Paceville.
Tel: 333640.*

Peppino's ££
Fashionable wine bar and restaurant.
Hot on pasta.
*Triq San Ġorġ (St George's Road),
St Julian's. Tel: 373200.*

Piccolo Padre £
Lively, well-decorated pizzeria belonging
to the Barracuda restaurant.
*195 Triq il-Kbira (Main Street),
St Julian's. Tel: 344875.*

San Guiliano ££££
Exceptional setting overlooking Spinola
Bay. Italian food; try the pasta with
cream, tomatoes and lobster.
*3 St Joseph's Street, Spinola Bay,
St Julian's. Tel: 231553.*

Upper Crust £
Cheap and cheerful pizza and pasta
house.

Floating restaurant – the *Black Pearl*

*4 Triq id-Dragunara (Dragonara Road),
Paceville. Tel: 373861.*

ST PAUL'S BAY
Gillieru ££££
Famous fish restaurant where film stars
and prime ministers have dined.
Triq il-Knisj (Church Street). Tel: 573480.

Le Pilier ££££
Inspired cuisine and a handsome setting
with arches and beams.
*14 Triq il-Mosta (Mosta Road).
Tel: 576887.*

Villa Mare £
No frills but good value; Friday night is
pasta night.
*Plazza tal-Bajja (Bay Square), Buġibba.
Tel: 573824.*

SLIEMA
The Carriage ££££
Sliema's best restaurant, combining
elegance and high-quality cuisine.
*68 Triq ix-Xatt (The Strand).
Tel: 333864/334584.*

Il-Fortizza £
Pizzeria/restaurant in a 19th-century
seafront fort.
Triq it-Torri (Tower Road). Tel: 336908.

Rendez-Vous £££
Popular and relatively smart spot for
Italian and French cuisine.
*55 Triq Dingli (Dingli Street). Tel:
337468. Closed: lunch except Sundays.*

Vino Veritas £
Café with classical music, open all day
for light meals, including vegetarian
dishes.
*59 Triq Dingli (Dingli Street). Tel:
342038.*

Winston's ££££
Well-known, and very expensive fish
restaurant.
*16–18 Triq il-Kbira (High Street).
Tel: 334584.*

VALLETTA
Bologna ₤₤₤
Good fresh pasta and other Italian fare.
59 Triq ir-Repubblika (Republic Street).
Tel: 246149.

Castille Restaurant ₤
Rooftop restaurant with harbour views and good wines.
Castille Hotel, Pjazza Kastilja (Castille Square). Tel: 243679.

Giannini ₤₤₤₤
International cuisine. High up on the bastions with magnificent harbour views.
23 Triq il-Mithna (Windmill Street).
Tel: 237121/236575.

Sicilia ₤
Simple, Sicilian-run restaurant with great views of Grand Harbour.
1a Triq San Gwann (St John Street).
Tel: 240569.

GOZO
GĦARB
Auberge Chez Amand ₤₤₤₤
Smart haunt of Gozitan and other gourmets who come for first-class French cuisine.
Triq Ta'Pinu (Ta'Pinu Street).
Tel: 551197.

Jeffrey's ₤
Simple and congenial little place serving pasta, rabbit, casseroles and fish.
10 Triq Għarb (Għarb Road).
Tel: 561006.

MARSALFORN
Auberge Ta'Frenċ ₤₤₤₤
Beautifully converted farmhouse in the countryside. Set meals are the best value.
Triq Marsalforn (Marsalforn Road).
Tel: 554668.

Victoria ₤
Simple and homely restaurant/bar run by a local artist and his wife.

Queen Victoria presides over the pavement cafés of Valletta's Republic Square

17 Triq ix-Xagħra (Xagħra Road).
Tel: 554646.

XAGĦRA
Oleander ₤
Meet the locals in this simple, friendly bar/restaurant on the village square.
10 Pjazza Victoria (Victory Square).
Tel: 557230.

XLENDI
It-Tmun ₤
Family-run, serving fresh fish or homemade dishes inside or out. Closed off season.
Trik il-Madonna tal-Karmnu (Mount Carmel Street). Tel 551571.

Paradise Bar/Restaurant ₤₤
Best known for its giant prawns and Elvis Presley *memorabilia*.
Triq il-Madonna tal-Karmnu (Mount Carmel Street). Tel: 556878.

Hotels and Accommodation

*I*n an effort to boost Malta's image, the government is injecting large sums of cash into the refurbishment of the island's 4- and 5-star hotels. In contrast to the over-ambitious building programme of the 1970s and '80s, when Malta looked perilously close to becoming a Spanish-costa style package destination, a complete stop has been put on new hotel developments.

All hotels in Malta, Gozo and Comino are graded from 5-star down to 1-star. Each hotel is inspected and classified by the Hotels and Catering Establishments Board, which is part of the Ministry of Tourism.

Generally speaking the grading of hotels is on facilities rather than style and character. Many 4-star hotels do not offer the same standards of service, comfort or décor that are demanded in the same category of hotel in most other European destinations. On the other

Modern hotel with views over Sliema's Ta'Xbiex marina

hand, they are a good deal cheaper.

The Malta National Tourism Organisation (see **Tourist Offices**, page 189) publishes an annual list of hotels, tourist villages and guest houses, giving guidance on facilities and the maximum amount that can be charged for accommodation in the middle to lower price bracket. Four- and 5-star hotels can charge what they like.

Prices

The prices given below indicate the cost of a twin room for one night, with continental breakfast. Although hotel rates are normally for bed and breakfast, most of them also offer half-board terms. These are often exceptional value, especially out of season.

Deluxe (Lm40–Lm80)

Malta only has a handful of hotels in this category and several of them, including the famous Corinthia Palace Hotel in Balzan (which claims it will be 'fit for kings and queens') are closed while they undergo comprehensive refurbishment.

Of those that are open, the 5-star Phoenicia is the oldest and grandest, built in colonial style and occupying a prime location over the Grand Harbour. In hotels of this category you can expect all the services that are commonplace in leading international hotels, including sports facilities, full air-conditioning and 24-hour room service.

Premier (Lm25–Lm45)

Four-star hotels provide a restaurant, a pool and air-conditioned rooms, but there is no guarantee of 24-hour room service or a television in individual rooms. Aware of current trends in health and fitness many hotels in this (as in the deluxe) category have added a gym and

In deluxe hotels like the Hilton International quality is taken for granted

sauna, plus leisure, beauty and/or fitness centres, in addition to offering sports facilities such as a pool. Bedrooms vary enormously, from standard 4-star comfort to surprisingly spartan décor and facilities.

Moderate (Lm18–25)

Many 3-star hotels are more akin to the European 2-star category. You can expect a restaurant, bar and rooms with en-suite bath or shower, but not necessarily a swimming pool. Sliema has the best choice in this category, while on Gozo the upgrading of hotels and the construction of new ones in the upmarket categories has left a dearth of decent middle-bracket accommodation.

Typical smaller hotel

Budget (Lm14–Lm20)

Malta has very few reasonably priced small hotels of charm and character. In the 1- and 2-star hotels you are not likely to find more than basic comforts. Rooms in 2-star hotels may or may not have en-suite shower rooms, while 1-star hotels will have communal bathrooms and handbasins in the bedrooms. The great majority have their own restaurants and offer half-board terms.

GUEST HOUSES

The names of Maltese guest houses – ranging from Fawlty Towers to The Ritz – are no indication of their real character. These are normally family-run establishments, categorised into first-, second- or third-class. A few in the first- and second-class categories have their own restaurants. Sliema has numerous guest houses and for those who want to get to know the Maltese (and perhaps try out some genuine Maltese home-cooked cuisine) a guest house has obvious advantages.

YOUTH HOSTELS

Hostels are divided into first-, second- and third-class categories. The Malta National Tourism Organisation guide lists half a dozen: five on Malta and one on Gozo. To obtain further information write to the Malta Youth Hostels Association at 17 Tal-Borġ Street, Paola, Malta.

HOTEL MEALS

Hotel breakfasts are normally of the continental type, consisting of coffee or tea, various breads and fruit juice. Hotels in the higher categories offer a buffet breakfast with extras such as cheese, ham, cereals and yoghurts. Main meals are normally of the 'international' variety, with perhaps a choice of one Maltese dish.

SELF-CATERING ACCOMMODATION

Malta has an abundance of self-catering accommodation, ranging from basic one-room studios to large apartments in huge holiday complexes, complete with their own pools, bars, shops, gym, restaurants and evening entertainment. The vast majority of these apartments and 'aparthotels' are located in Sliema, St Julian's, Qawra and Buġibba. Many tour operators feature this type of accommodation in their package holidays to Malta.

The Hotels and Catering Establishments Board fixes maximum prices for this accommodation and can provide a list of all the self-catering units in the islands (write to the Board at 280 Republic Street, Valletta, Malta, CMR 02). If you arrive without prior booking, the local tourist offices (see page 189) will give you addresses of apartments and villas to rent in their area. Alternatively you can look in the columns of the Maltese English-language newspaper, *The Times*.

By contrast with the big and anonymous apartment blocks there are several more exclusive holiday villages. Here accommodation is provided in bungalows, villas or low-rise apartment blocks and the facilities include swimming pools, a restaurant and a sports centre. Examples include the Mistra Village, overlooking St Paul's Bay and the Club Nautico hotel/apartment complex on the island of Comino.

Renting a converted farmhouse is becoming increasingly popular, particularly on Gozo. The Cornucopia Hotel in Xagħra offers a choice of well-equipped farmhouses and guests can use the hotel facilities. There are also farmhouses to rent in Sannat, Għarb, Xewkija, Xagħra and Żebbuġ.

THOMAS COOK
Traveller's Tip

Travellers who purchase their travel tickets from Thomas Cook are entitled to use the services of any Thomas Cook network location, free of charge, to make hotel reservations.

Peak holiday times for the Maltese islands are from May to September, Christmas, Carnival (the weekend before Lent) and Easter. You are advised to make your reservation well in advance if you are visiting at these times.

Most hotels offer a swimming pool

On Business

*F*oreign investment is actively being sought by Malta and the government has introduced various incentives for companies considering manufacturing on the islands, including tax exemptions and subsidised factory rents. Several major infrastructural projects are scheduled for the 1990s, including a new airport terminal, the overhaul of the telecommunications system and the upgrading of hotels. A stock exchange – the smallest in the world – was opened in February 1992 and in 1988 the Malta International Financial and Business Authority was set up specifically to promote the islands as an offshore financial centre.

BUSINESS ETIQUETTE

There are no rigid rules of formality though the normal social courtesies, the right dress and forms of address, will go a long way. The Maltese shake hands on meeting and parting. Business cards are always appreciated.

Reasonably smart dress is expected for business. If in doubt err on the conservative side. Men should wear a suit or jacket and tie; women should appear elegant, though this does not necessarily mean wearing a conventional suit.

Business visits often involve the exchange of small gifts (and the greasing of palms is not unknown). If you are invited to a private home, take flowers, chocolates or a bottle of wine. Refusing hospitality from a Maltese, whether a drink or a homemade dessert at the end of a Maltese meal, is likely to cause offence.

BUSINESS HOURS

Government working hours differ according to the season: in summer (16 June to 30 September) they are Monday to Friday 7.30am–1.30pm; in winter they are from 7.45am–5.15pm, with a one-hour break for lunch.

The hours of private companies are normally Monday to Friday 8.30am–5pm all year round, with a one- to two-hour lunch break. Some businesses, however, start earlier in the summer and work through until the early afternoon.

CONFERENCE AND EXHIBITION SITES

The **Mediterranean Conference Centre** was converted from the Sacra Infirmeria, the Old Hospital of the Knights of St John (see page 41), and is the most splendid conference centre on the islands. The historic atmosphere, combined with modern amenities, attracts conferences, meetings and exhibitions from all over the world (tel: 243840 for further information).

The **Eden Palladium** (tel: 319899/341191), Malta's only nightclub, is also a venue for conferences and product launches. Most of the island's 4- and 5-star hotels offer facilities. Information regarding conference and incentive travel is available from the Malta National Tourism Organisation (see **Tourist Offices**, page 189).

MALTA INTERNATIONAL TRADE FAIR

The Malta International Trade Fair and other exhibitions are held in the grounds

The Mediterranean Conference Centre, formerly the Knights' Hospital

of the Palazzo Parisio in Naxxar (tel: 410371).

MEDIA

Malta's one English-language daily newspaper, *The Times*, gives business news. Major European newspapers arrive in Malta on the same day of publication. *The Economic Update* is a local magazine, published monthly.

SECRETARIAL AND OFFICE SERVICES

Most of the 5-star hotels offer secretarial services. A number of companies specialise in providing secretarial services, such as typing, binding and sending faxes. **Secretarial Services Ltd**, BOV Centre, Triq Irjali (High Street), Sliema (tel: 336507).

TELECOMMUNICATIONS

The Telemalta offices, at various locations on Malta and Gozo (see **Telephones**, page 188) provide telephone, fax, telex, and telegram services.

TRANSLATION SERVICES

A number of companies provide translation services, of variable quality. **International Translation Agency**, 15 Triq Sant'Antnin (St Anthony Street), Sliema (tel: 319008).

USEFUL ADDRESSES

The Malta International Financial Business Authority provides brochures on the benefits, advantages and opportunities of setting up international financial and trading activities from within Malta. Palazzo Spinola, St Julian's, Malta (tel: 344230, fax: 344334). The Malta National Tourism Organisation has a Conference and Incentive Bureau. Information is available from their offices abroad or from the head office at 280 Triq ir-Repubblika (Republic Street), Valletta, CMR 02 (tel: 224444/5; fax: 220401).

Practical Guide

ARRIVING

Entry formalities

Citizens from the UK, EC countries, the US, Canada, Australia and New Zealand may enter Malta for up to three months without a visa. Only a standard passport is required. British nationals may also travel on a visitor's passport. Visitors from South Africa will need a visa.

By air

Luqa international airport is located 6km south of Valletta. The new international terminal, which opened in 1992, offers a wide range of facilities: 24-hour currency exchange services, car-hire desks, a tourist information office, a restaurant, a variety of shops, a runway viewing area and even live musical entertainment on Sundays. For flight enquiries tel: 249600. To confirm return flight reservations tel: 882921 at least 24 hours prior to departure.

Buses 8 and 39 link the airport with Valletta. Alternatively there are plenty of taxis.

Air Malta operates a scheduled service from many European destinations, including London, Manchester, Paris, Amsterdam, Rome and Frankfurt. The airline also operates charter services from a number of British airports. Air Malta has offices in Valletta at 11–12 Freedom Square (tel: 240686) and at 285 Republic Street (tel: 234397); and in Sliema at 28 Tower Road (tel: 316242).

By sea

The **Gozo Channel Company** (tel: 243964) operates a car ferry service between Malta and Catania in Sicily. The journey time is 8 hours. **Virtu Rapid Ferries** (3 Princess Elizabeth Street, Ta'Xbiex, Malta, tel: 317088) offers a high-speed passenger-only catamaran service from Sicily to Malta, reducing the journey time to one hour 40 minutes.

Air Malta operates between the island and many European capitals

The Italian line, **Tirrenia**, operates a regular service from Malta to Syracuse, Catania and Reggio Calabria, and a weekly crossing from Naples.

CAMPING
There are no camping or caravan sites on Malta.

CHILDREN
Undercurrents are quite common and parents should keep a wary eye on children who swim in the sea. Great care should be also be taken to prevent children getting badly sunburnt.

An abundance of casual cafés serving pizzas, hamburgers, and chips makes eating out with children an easy affair. For self-caterers, mini-markets sell familiar brands of foods as well as baby foods and nappies.

CLIMATE
The average temperature is over 22°C. The really hot months are from June to September when temperatures can soar to 32°C or more. Sea breezes bring welcome relief from the heat. Less welcome is the *xlokk* or *sirocco* wind, which blows from the Sahara, raising the

temperature and bringing high humidity. Autumn is warm, though storms and rain are quite frequent, particularly in October. In winter the weather varies from warm and sunny to periods when it is cold, wet and windy. Spring, which is generally considered the best time to go to Malta, is warm and sunny and the countryside is covered in wild flowers.

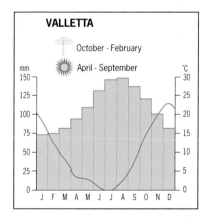

VALLETTA

October - February

April - September

mm   °C

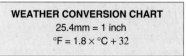

WEATHER CONVERSION CHART
25.4mm = 1 inch
°F = 1.8 × °C + 32

CONVERSION TABLES
See opposite.

CRIME
There are very few cases of serious crime on Malta and nowhere on the island are you likely to feel threatened. Instances of theft are comparatively low. Most involve breaking in to hired cars, and there are occasional instances of bag snatching. At night it is best to avoid Strait Street (the red-light quarter) in Valletta, as well as the Gzira suburb and the Three Cities.

CUSTOMS REGULATIONS
The duty-free allowance for visitors to Malta is 200 cigarettes (or the equivalent in cigars or tobacco), one litre of spirits or two litres of fortified wine, one bottle of perfume and 125g of toilet water.

DISABLED TRAVELLERS
Rocky beaches, steep streets and sites with numerous steps mean that Malta is a challenge for the disabled. Valletta, Mdina and Victoria (on Gozo) are particularly tricky for wheelchairs. Few museums have facilities for the disabled though some prehistoric sites are accessible. For information on facilities for the handicapped in Malta contact the Health Educational Unit (tel: 231247) or the National Commission for the Handicapped (tel: 487789). The hotel guide published by the Malta National Tourism Organisation (see **Tourist Offices**, page 189) indicates which hotels have facilities for the disabled.

DRIVING
Malta's principal driving hazard consists of local drivers who are renowned for overtaking on blind bends, hogging the middle of the road (or your side if it happens to be in the shade) and

Motoring *memorabilia* – a relic of the British administration of Malta

assuming that they have the right-of-way on roundabouts and at crossroads. Other drawbacks are the potholed roads and poor signposting, particularly on Malta. A golden rule is to remember that all petrol stations are shut on Sunday.

Car hire
Malta is one of the cheapest places in Europe to hire a car. Local law permits driving from 18 years and there is no upper age limit. Even so, some companies will not hire cars to those aged under 25 or over 70, while others will charge extra daily insurance for doing so. Drivers must present their own national driving licence or an internationally recognised driving licence. There is an additional charge

for any extra driver. The main international car-hire companies have desks at the airport as well as in the major resorts. Local companies are cheaper, but their cars may not be quite as reliable as those of the well-known companies. Among the more reliable local car-hire companies are:

John's, 35 Sliema Road, Gzira (tel: 334849).

Driveaway, 1 Nicolo Isouard Street, Sliema (tel: 331105).

Mexico Car Rentals, St Philip Street, Birżebbuġa (tel: 828625).

Breakdowns

The normal procedure in the case of a breakdown is to call the police on 191 (562040/4 in Gozo) and stay with the car. For most insurance claims a police report is crucial. In the event of a breakdown call the car-hire company for assistance.

Parking

Parking on pavements or any available slot, legal or illegal, is common practice. Notoriously difficult places to park, particularly in summer, are Valletta and Mdina.

Petrol

Petrol or gas is sold by the litre. Service stations close at 7pm in summer, 6pm in winter, and all of them are closed on Sundays and holidays. Not all service stations sell unleaded petrol, which most hired cars run on.

Regulations

Driving is on the left. The speed limit is 64kph on highways and 40kph in built-up areas. Cars approaching a roundabout must give way to the traffic already on the circuit (in theory).

Conversion Table

FROM	TO	MULTIPLY BY
Inches	Centimetres	2.54
Feet	Metres	0.3048
Yards	Metres	0.9144
Miles	Kilometres	1.6090
Acres	Hectares	0.4047
Gallons	Litres	4.5460
Ounces	Grams	28.35
Pounds	Grams	453.6
Pounds	Kilograms	0.4536
Tons	Tonnes	1.0160

To convert back, for example from centimetres to inches, divide by the number in the the third column.

Men's Suits

UK	36	38	40	42	44	46	48
Rest of Europe	46	48	50	52	54	56	58
US	36	38	40	42	44	46	48

Dress Sizes

UK	8	10	12	14	16	18
France	36	38	40	42	44	46
Italy	38	40	42	44	46	48
Rest of Europe	34	36	38	40	42	44
US	6	8	10	12	14	16

Men's Shirts

UK	14	14.5	15	15.5	16	16.5	17
Rest of Europe	36	37	38	39/40	41	42	43
US	14	14.5	15	15.5	16	16.5	17

Men's Shoes

UK	7	7.5	8.5	9.5	10.5	11
Rest of Europe	41	42	43	44	45	46
US	8	8.5	9.5	10.5	11.5	12

Women's Shoes

UK	4.5	5	5.5	6	6.5	7
Rest of Europe	38	38	39	39	40	41
US	6	6.5	7	7.5	8	8.5

ELECTRICITY
240 volts, 50 cycles. Three-pin square British-style plugs are used.

EMBASSIES AND CONSULATES
Australia Australian High Commission, Ta'Xbiex Terrace, Ta'Xbiex (tel: 338201/5).
Canada Canadian Consulate, 103 Archbishop Street, Valletta (tel: 233122). The nearest embassy is in Rome (tel: (396) 844 1841).
New Zealand The nearest embassy is in Rome (tel: (396) 440 2928).
UK British High Commission, 7 St Anne Street, Floriana (tel: 233134).
US American Embassy, Development House, St Anne Street, Floriana (tel: 240425).

EMERGENCY TELEPHONE NUMBERS
Ambulance 196 (199 on Gozo)
Fire 199
Police 191
St Luke's Hospital, Gwardamanġa, Malta 241251.
Thomas Cook Travellers' Cheque emergency refund number (in case of lost or stolen travellers's cheques) tel: 0044 733 502995 (24-hour service – reverse the charges).

HEALTH
Visitors from Australia, the US, Canada and Europe do not require certificates of vaccination or inoculation to enter Malta. The standard of medical treatment on the islands is generally very good. Malta has reciprocal health care agreements with Australia, Belgium, Bulgaria, Czechoslovakia, Greece, Hungary, Poland, Turkey and the UK. Visitors from these countries staying for up to a month are entitled to free medical and hospital treatment in Malta and Gozo. The main hospital on Malta is St Luke's in Gwardamanġa, on the outskirts of Valletta (tel: 241251); on Gozo, it is the Craig Hospital in Victoria (tel: 561600). As well as hospitals, there are the government health centres in towns and large villages. If you need a doctor urgently, ask your hotel or go to the nearest pharmacy. Anyone taking medicines into Malta or wanting to purchase fresh supplies locally is advised to take a letter of introduction from their doctor. The water in Malta is perfectly safe to drink.

INSURANCE
Travel insurance should be taken out to cover you against theft, loss of property and medical expenses.

MAPS
Tourist offices provide free plans of Valletta, Buġibba and Sliema, plus a basic island map. The Mid-Med Bank and Bank of Valletta also give out very basic maps of the islands.

MEDIA
The standard of newspaper reporting is high. The local English-language daily paper is *The Times*, which leans slightly to the right of centre. Another local English-language paper, *The Sunday Times*, is exceptionally good, though there is competition now from the newly formed *Independent*, also published on Sunday. In Valletta and Sliema major foreign newspapers are usually available on the day of publication. On Gozo foreign newspapers arrive on the following day. The fortnightly tourist guide *What's On in Malta and Gozo* is packed with information on what to see and do. It is available from book and

LANGUAGE

English is spoken almost everywhere you go and it is not necessary to know any Maltese (or Malti). It does help, however, if you can master basic pronunciation, particularly for place names which sound very different to the way they look. The following is a basic and approximate guide to the pronunciation of those letters which cause the most confusion.

Maltese English

ċ - ch

ġ - j

għ - silent

h - silent, except at the end of a word when it is aspirated

ħ - h

j - y

m - m, except if the initial M is followed by a consonant, when it becomes im. (Mdina is therefore imDEEnah).

q - silent

x - sh

ż - tz

For those who feel tempted to give Maltese a go, here are a few basic phrases.

yes	**iva**
no	**le**
please	**jekk joghġbok**
thank you	**grazzi**
good morning	**bonġu**
good evening	**bonswa**
goodbye	**saħħa**
How are you?	**kif int?**
excuse me	**skużi**
How much?	**kemm?**
What is your name?	**X'ismek?**
My name is...	**Jisimni...**
Where is?	**Fejn hu?**
right	**lemin**
left	**xellug**

The following are useful if you are touring. Many of the words appear on maps.

cave	**għar**
spring, well	**għajn**
inlet, harbour	**marsa**
sandy bay	**ramla**
cliff	**rdum**
headland	**ras**
valley, gorge	**wied**
tower	**borġ**
viewpoint	**nadur**

souvenir shops. Radio Malta broadcasts in both Maltese and English. The BBC World Service can be picked up on short wave. For light radio 24 hours a day, Island Sound broadcasts on FM101.8.

The local television channel shows many films and programmes in English and transmits a daily news bulletin.

MONEY MATTERS

The unit of currency is the Maltese lira (Lm), divided into 100 cents and each cent in turn divided into 10 mils. Notes come in denominations of Lm20, Lm10, Lm5 and L2; coins in Lm1, 50c, 25c, 10c, 5c, 2c and 1c. Mil coins (5m, 3m and 2m) are rapidly becoming obsolete.

Any amount of foreign currency can be brought into Malta, but the import of local currency is restricted to Lm50. Unlimited quantities of foreign currency can be taken out of Malta but the export of local currency is restricted to Lm25.

Major credit cards, travellers' cheques and Eurocheques, backed by a guarantee card, are all widely accepted. Holders   of Visa cards can withdraw cash at cashpoints in Malta and Gozo. Foreign cash is accepted in many shops.

The two major banks, Mid-Med Bank and the Bank of Valletta, have branches all over the island. Banks are open Monday to Friday from 8am–noon or 8.30am–noon (some also open on Friday afternoon) and on Saturday from 8–11.30am or 8.30am–noon. Foreign exchange facilities at banks normally stay open for the afternoon. There are 24-hour bank exchange facilities at Luqa Airport all year round. The main hotels will exchange foreign currency but at rates less favourable than those of banks.

Thomas Cook

Thomas Cook (see page 189 for offices) will exchange your currency and cash your travellers' cheques. No commission is charged for changing foreign cash. For travellers' cheques Thomas Cook gives the most favourable rates on Malta. No commission is levied on Thomas Cook MasterCard Travellers' Cheques and emergency assistance is provided in the case of their loss or theft.

NATIONAL HOLIDAYS

On the following dates offices, museums, monuments and most shops will be closed.

1 January New Year's Day
10 February Feast of St Paul's Shipwreck
19 March Feast of St Joseph
31 March Freedom Day
Variable Good Friday
1 May Workers' Day
7 June Commemoration of 7 June 1919
29 June Feast of St Peter and St Paul
15 August Feast of the Assumption
8 September Victory Day
21 September Independence Day
8 December Feast of the Immaculate Conception
13 December Republic Day
25 December Christmas Day.

Filling up at the petrol station

OPENING HOURS

Shops

Shops are normally open 9am–7pm with a three- or four-hour lunch break. Most shops close on Sundays and public holidays, though a few stay open on Sunday mornings.

Museums

The majority of museums are government-run and have standard opening hours.
In Malta these are:
16 June to 30 September – daily
7.45am–2pm, Sunday 8am–1.45pm;
1 October to 15 June – daily
8.15am–5pm, Sunday 8.15am–4pm.
In Gozo the opening times are:
1 April to 15 June: Monday to Saturday
8.30am–6.30pm (Sunday 3pm);
16 June to 15 September, Monday to
Saturday 8.30am–7pm (Sunday 3pm),
16–30 September until 6.30pm;
1 October to 31 March, Monday to
Saturday 8.30am–4.30pm (Sunday 3pm).

ORGANISED TOURS

Several companies offer a selection of fully guided tours of the islands. Prices compare favourably with excursions in other parts of Europe but your enjoyment will depend largely on the enthusiasm and energy of your guide. If you want to explore Valletta and Mdina you will probably get more enjoyment by going independently and browsing at your leisure. For those without a car the full-day island tours are a good way of seeing the highlights. When making a reservation, check if the price includes the boat trip to the Blue Grotto – some companies don't warn you of this extra, and quite substantial, cost.

Captain Morgan has the monopoly on cruises, ranging from harbour tours to a full-day cruise around the Maltese islands (for details see page 156).

One- and two-day excursions are offered to Sicily.

PHARMACIES

Pharmacists are well qualified and Maltese pharmacies (also called chemists) are stocked with most well-known brands of medicines. They keep normal shop opening times from Monday to Saturday. On Sundays they open on a roster basis, one in each district and for the morning only. Consult *The Sunday Times* for details.

PLACES OF WORSHIP

The Maltese are devoutly Catholic but all religions are tolerated. Mass is generally celebrated in Maltese but in Valletta, Sliema, St Julian's, Rabat, St Paul's Bay and Mellieħa, there are services in English on Sunday mornings. For details, see the magazine *What's On in Malta and Gozo* or the weekend papers. Church of England services are held in Valletta at St Paul's Anglican Cathedral and the Bible Baptist Church, and in Sliema, at the Holy Trinity Church.

POLICE

The police headquarters is in Floriana, tel: 224001. The police wear a black uniform in winter, and khaki in summer. The number for police on Gozo is 562040 or 562044.

POST OFFICE

The Maltese postal service is cheap and efficient. Stamps can be bought at post offices, most hotels, newsagents and many shops.

The General Post Office occupies the Auberge d'Italie, Merchants' Street,

One of the island's venerable old buses

Valletta. The opening hours are Monday to Saturday 7.30am–6pm in summer, 8am–6.30pm in winter, and on Sundays all year from 8am–noon. A *poste restante* service is available. There are branch offices at Manwel Dimech Street, Sliema; 21 Wilga Street, Paceville, St Julian's; Islets Promenade, Buġibba.

The Gozo branches are at: 129 Republic Street, Victoria; St Anthony Street, Mġarr.

PUBLIC TRANSPORT
Bus

The bus service on Malta offers an extremely cheap and efficient way of touring the island. The only drawback – unless you happen to be staying in Valletta – is that nearly all buses start and end up in the capital. The old British Bedford and Leyland buses rattle along at surprising speed, but these lovable and antiquated old vehicles are gradually being replaced by more sophisticated, softer-seated and quieter models.

The bus terminus at City Gate, Valletta, is daunting for the uninitiated and the information kiosk is not conspicuous. The buses, which throng around the monumental Triton Fountain, are marked with a number, but no destination. Once you have established the number you want (there is a list up at City Gate), you must then search among dozens of similar-looking buses for the right one. The quickest way to find what you want is just to ask one of the drivers.

Tickets are bought from the bus driver as you board. Children under 10 travel half price. The longest journey on the island is no more than 40 minutes (traffic permitting) and the average is between 20 and 30 minutes. The last

buses of the day run at the relatively early time of 9pm or 9.30pm.

Buses on Gozo, radiating from Victoria, are not so reliable. You can, however, depend on bus 25, the one that meets the ferry at Mġarr and takes you to Victoria (and, in summer, Marsalforn and Xlendi). Always keep small change for the bus driver.

Dgħajsa

The *dgħajsa*, pronounced 'dicer', is a brightly coloured water-taxi which, when manoeuvred by a standing oarsman, is reminiscent of the Venetian gondola. The majority now have outboard motors and are used to transport tourists across Grand Harbour to the Three Cities. The departure point is the Customs House wharf in Valletta. Return boats leave from the waterfront at Senglea or Vittoriosa. This charming form of transport is not cheap, so you should be prepared to bargain.

Ferries

The Gozo Channel Company operates a car and passenger ferry service between Ċirkewwa in Malta and Mġarr in Gozo (in Malta tel: 580435; in Gozo tel: 556114; for a recorded timetable tel: 556016).

The timetables are subject to change without notice and the crossings are dependent on weather conditions. In really bad weather the boats leave from St Paul's Bay. If the seas look at all rough it is worth ringing to check whether the ferry is running at all. Passengers with cars should arrive in good time, particularly in summer. There are no advanced reservations and queues can soon build up.

The cost depends on whether you are Maltese, Gozitan or non-resident. The Maltese pay more than the Gozitans and visitors more than the Maltese. However, even the tourist rate is good value for this enjoyable journey which lasts around 20 to 25 minutes.

The Gozo Channel Company also operates a service to Gozo from Sa Maison pier at Pieta Creek, Valletta. This is limited to one crossing a day, from Monday to Friday. The journey time is 75 minutes. A hovermarine service on the same route takes just 25 minutes. Sliema (25 minutes) and Buġibba (15 minutes) also have hovermarine services to Gozo.

Helicopter

Thirteen-seat helicopters operate a service from Luqa airport on Malta to the heliport near Xewkija on Gozo. The journey takes 10 minutes. Alternatively you can take 20- or 40-minute sightseeing trips of the Maltese islands or an all-day package to Gozo with car-hire and lunch included. Reservations can be made through any travel agent or Air Malta (tel: 882920).

A gentle way to travel – pony cart trotting through the rural lanes of central Malta

Karrozzin

The *karrozzin* is a quaint horse-drawn cab, which, when your feet are weary, will take you at a gentle pace through the streets of Valletta, Sliema or Mdina. In Valletta they wait at City Gate, Great Siege Square, the Customs House and at various points along the bastions. Always drive a hard bargain with a *karrozzin* driver.

Motorbikes and bicycles

The hills, hot climate, potholes and general lack of facilities for cyclists don't make for ideal biking conditions on Malta or Gozo. Even so, bicycles and motor bikes can be hired throughout the islands at reasonable rents.

Cycle Store, 135 Eucharistic Congress Street, Mosta (tel: 443235); bicycles only.

Peter's Scooter Shop, Peter Azzopardi, 175a D'Argens Road, Msida (tel: 335244); motorbikes only.

Victor Sultana, New Building, Main Gate Street, Victoria, Gozo (tel: 556414); motorbikes and bikes.

Taxis

Taxis are readily available at the airport, in Valletta (at City Gate and Palace Square), in Sliema (on the Strand) and at other main tourist centres. The white taxis with red number plates can be hailed in the street. These all have meters but they are not always used and overcharging is not unknown. The black taxis are private and must be hired by phone. For a reliable 24-hour service, try Wembley's at 50 St George's Road, St Julian's, (tel: 311522).

SENIOR CITIZENS

The only discount available to senior citizens is on museum entrance fees. Unlike EC countries there is no upper age limit for hiring a car (though some hire companies are reluctant to hire out to over-70s).

Malta attracts a large number of older visitors and many tour operators specialise in holidays for them, notably Saga Holidays.

Saga Holidays Ltd, Saga Building, Middelburg Square, Folkestone, Kent, CT20 1AZ, UK (tel: 0800–300600).

Saga International, 120 Boylton Street, Boston, Massachusetts 02116 (tel: 617–451 6808).

TELEPHONES

Malta's British-style coin-only telephone kiosks are gradually giving way to new Telemalta phone-card booths. These greatly facilitate telephoning abroad. Telecards can be purchased from any Telemalta branch or other outlets carrying the Telecard sign.

Overseas telephone calls can also be made from Telemalta's offices at the following addresses, which also offer fax and telegram services:

Mercury House, St George's Road, St

Julian's (main office). Open: 24 hours.
South Street, Valletta. Open: weekdays
8.30am–6.30pm.
Bisazza Street, Sliema. Open: weekdays
8.30am–11pm.
Luqa Airport. Open: 24 hours.
St Paul's Street, St Paul's Bay. Open:
weekdays 8.30am–11pm.
Republic Street, Victoria, Gozo. Open:
daily 8.30am–11pm.

The international telephone codes are:
Australia 0061
Ireland 00353
New Zealand 0064
UK 0044
US and **Canada** 001.

Overseas operator tel: 194.
Local enquiries tel: 190.
Cheap rates for calling abroad are
Monday to Saturday 9pm–8am and all
day Sunday.
    International calls from shops or hotel
telephones cost considerably more than
those made from public telephones or
the Telemalta offices.
    Telecell (tel: 482820) offers short
term rental of mobile telephones.

THOMAS COOK SERVICES
Thomas Cook has offices at Il-Piazzetta,
Tower Road, Sliema (tel: 344225, fax:
342273) and at 20, Republic Street,
Valletta (tel: 235948, fax: 235951).
    The Thomas Cook Worldwide
Customer Promise offers free emergency
assistance at any Thomas Cook Network
location to travellers who have purchased
their travel tickets at a Thomas Cook
location.

TIME
Malta time is one hour ahead of
Greenwich Mean Time (GMT) in winter

and two hours ahead in summer (last
weekend of March to last weekend of
September). During Standard Time
periods, when it is noon in Malta, it is
9pm in Sydney, 11pm in Auckland, 6am
in New York and Montreal and 11am in
London.

TIPPING
Tipping is not entirely necessary but will
always be appreciated. All restaurants
automatically include a 10 per cent
service charge on the bill but it is normal
to leave a little extra if the service
deserves it. Taxi-drivers don't necessarily
expect to be tipped. Car park attendants
at free car parks in popular sites will
hover around your car, hoping for a few
cents.

TOILETS
The toilets of bars and cafés, if they exist
at all, are often surprisingly dirty, with no
paper or soap. Public toilets are a better
bet.

TOURIST OFFICES
The head office of the Malta National
Tourism Organisation is at 280 Republic
Street, Valletta, CMR 02 (tel: 238282 or
224444/5). Tourist information offices
are located at:
1 City Gate, Valletta, tel: 237747.
Luqa Airport, tel: 249600 ext 6073.
Bisazza Street, Sliema, tel: 313409.
Main Street, Balluta, tel: 342671.
    The Gozo tourist information offices
are at:
Mġarr Harbour, tel: 553343.
Republic Street, Victoria, tel: 558106.
    The Malta National Tourism
Organisation in London is at:
Mappin House, Suite 300, 4 Winsley
Street, London W1N 7AR, tel: 071-323
0506.

ACKNOWLEDGEMENTS

The Automobile Association wishes to thank the following organisations, libraries and photographers for their assistance in the preparation of this book.

J ALLAN CASH PHOTOLIBRARY 69, 98; ARDEA LONDON 146 (P Morris), 163c (P Morris); MALTA NATIONAL TOURIST OFFICE 38, 72/3, 72, 73, 99, 144, 163b, 177; MARY EVANS PICTURE LIBRARY 10/11, 35a, b; NATURE PHOTOGRAPHERS LTD 87 (M Gore); PHOENICIAN GLASS WORKS, MALTA 148; RAF MUSEUM, HENDON 20; SPECTRUM COLOUR LIBRARY 100, 114, 161; THE TRAVEL LIBRARY 31, (D Cilia), 37 (D Cilia), 40 (D Cilia), 54 (P Enticknap), 58 (D Cilia), 59 (D Cilia), 65 (P Enticknap), 81 (P Enticknap), 112 (D Cilia), 135 (D Cilia), 136 (P Enticknap); ZEFA PICTURE LIBRARY (UK) LTD inset, spine, 145.

The remaining photographs are held in the AA Photo Library with contributions from:

P Enticknap Cover, 1, 2, 4, 12, 14, 15, 17, 18, 19, 21b, d, 22, 23, 28, 29, 32, 33, 35, 36, 42, 43, 44, 45, 51b, 52, 55, 56, 60, 66, 67a, b, 68, 76, 78, 81, 84, 85, 88, 89, 90, 91b, 92, 95a, b, 96, 97, 101a, b, 102, 103, 104, 106, 108, 109, 115, 124, 129, 130, 131, 132, 134, 137, 140, 141, 142, 149, 150, 152, 153, 155, 157, 160, 162, 164, 165, 166a, b, 167a, b, 170, 171, 172, 173; 175, 179, 180, 186.

D Vincent 63, 77, 126, 128, 147, 185, 187, 188.

W Voysey 5, 9, 13, 16, 21a, c, 24, 25, 34, 39, 41, 50, 51a, 61, 62, 64, 70, 71, 74, 75, 79, 86a, b, 91a, 93, 94, 107, 111, 113, 117, 119, 120, 121, 127, 133, 139, 143, 146, 151, 156, 159, 163a, 169, 174, 183, 184.

The author would like to thank the National Tourism Organisation of Malta, London; Air Malta, UK and Christina Farrugia, Thomas Cook, Malta.

The Automobile Association would also like to thank Mr Kenneth De Martino, Thomas Cook Malta Ltd for his help.

Series adviser: Melissa Shales

Edited by Christopher Catling